POETRY COM[P]

GREAT MINDS

Your World...Your Future...YOUR WORDS

From Surrey Vol II
Edited by Steve Twelvetree

First published in Great Britain in 2005 by:
Young Writers
Remus House
Coltsfoot Drive
Peterborough
PE2 9JX
Telephone: 01733 890066
Website: www.youngwriters.co.uk

All Rights Reserved

© *Copyright Contributors 2005*

SB ISBN 1 84602 075 1

Foreword

This year, the Young Writers' 'Great Minds' competition proudly presents a showcase of the best poetic talent selected from over 40,000 up-and-coming writers nationwide.

Young Writers was established in 1991 to promote the reading and writing of poetry within schools and to the youth of today. Our books nurture and inspire confidence in the ability of young writers and provide a snapshot of poems written in schools and at home by budding poets of the future.

The thought, effort, imagination and hard work put into each poem impressed us all and the task of selecting poems was a difficult but nevertheless enjoyable experience.

We hope you are as pleased as we are with the final selection and that you and your family continue to be entertained with *Great Minds From Surrey Vol II* for many years to come.

Contents

Coombe Girls' School
Natasha Dawes (12)	1
Natasha Hussey (12)	2
Venice Byatt (13)	2
Reed Thomas-Litman (13)	3
Charlene Edwards (13)	3
Charlotte McVay (13)	4
Sarah Fry (14)	5
Amy Green (13)	6
Katie Proudlove (12)	6
Sarah Eastop (12)	7
Abby Keaveney (13)	7
Emily Britton (13)	8
Rosalie Vanderpant (12)	8
Flynn Thomas-Litman (12)	9
Laura Sowell (12)	9
Elekia Akhuetie (12)	10
Tessa Tyler Todd (12)	10
Rashel Rassapour (12)	11
Antoaneta Roussinova (13)	11
Jessica Archard (13)	12
Emily Powell (12)	12
Aiswarya Sivagnanam (13)	13
Hatice Resa (12)	14
Lizzie Foulds (12)	14
Kayantha Sivalingam (12)	15
Emma Weston (12)	15
Kirstyn Luton (12)	16
Sophie Croft (11)	17
Laura Burrows (11)	18
Xoana Rodriguez (11)	18
Shareen Hearn (13)	19
Francesca Jacques (12)	20
Apoorva Khosti (12)	20
Georgina Edwards (11)	21
Jahdine Milosevic (13)	21
Ella Edey (11)	22
Hana Al-Amiri (13)	22
Anna Driscoll (11)	23

Tessa Lloyd (11)	23
Sian Macarty Cole (12)	24
Amelia Bradley (12)	25
Claudia Adolphus (11)	25
Kiran Bejawn (12)	26
Chanel Cullen (12)	27
Emma Brown (12)	28
Beryl Kumpha (12)	28
Bijal Bhundia (12)	29
Georgia Sergant (11)	29
Sarah Dyson (12)	30
Morsal Sherzad (13)	31
Emily Patton (12)	32
Amy Lawrence (12)	33
Jennie Murchie (13)	33
Zena Daniel (13)	34
Shaista Kerai (11)	35
Lucy Brown (12)	36
Jeong-Inn Kim (13)	37
Poppy Newman (11)	38
Emily Finch (11)	39
Yeah-Been Suh (12)	40
Rosina Martin (12)	41
Nan Pancoast (12)	42
Eujean Cha (12)	43
Emily Warland (13)	44
Rhian Bamsey (13)	45
Stephanie Tizzard (13)	46
Nicole Davies (13)	46
Katherine Adams (12)	47
Alexandra Wright (11)	47
Lindsay Sivakumar (11)	48
Candace Grigsby (13)	49
Amy House (11)	49
Suzie Robson (11)	50
Victoria Bradley (12)	51
Charmaine Whitcombe (14)	52
Nicola Giles (11)	52
Hannah Wheatley (13)	53

Glenthorne High School

Charlie Henthorn (12)	53
Emma Wooldridge (12)	54
Christopher Emmerson (12)	54
Hayley Cahill (11)	55
Laura Knight (12)	55
Sam Connoley (13)	56
James Craig (13)	56
Gabriel Mallows (11)	57
Ben Healy (12)	57
Andrew Bragg (12)	58
Megan Pattwell (11)	58
Courtney Porter (13)	59
Leslie Apeah (12)	59
Daniel McNamara (13)	60
Laura-Jayne Lawton (11)	60
Danielle Connor (13)	61
George Tribe (11)	61
Lauren Lewis (13)	62
Dean Stone (13)	63
Vivek Sharma (13)	64
Stacey Noble (12)	65
Leigh Henthorn (13)	66
John Casey (12)	66
Sheriece Bracey (12)	67
Katy Godbeer (12)	67
Stacey McDougall (12)	68
Shauna Curran (14)	68
Lewis Sawyers (12)	68
Becky Wisdom (13)	69
Rachel Stannard (12)	69
Abbie Studholme (12)	69
George Hellewell (11)	70
Lucas Willmott (12)	70
Caroline Flinders (13)	71
Thomas Yelf (13)	71
Jamie Hall (12)	72
Megan Thoroughgood (12)	72
Hannah Jeffries (13)	73
Daniel Gregory (13)	73
Lauren Payne (13)	74

Dakordass Tengur (13)	75
Hannah Whitehead (11)	76
Russell Wells (13)	76
Megan King (12)	77
Chris Sayers (12)	77
Jamie Clayton (13)	78
Anthony Fagan (13)	79
Sean Murphy (12)	80
Kiran Williams (13)	80
Michelle Easton (12)	81
Scott Nicholls (12)	81
Emily Bullimore (12)	82
Jo Hannah (13)	82
Harry Knock (12)	82
Holly Ellemarie Richards (11)	83
Daniel Kyprianou (12)	83
Sara Druce (12)	83
Alex Dawson (12)	84
Vida Kohan Ghadr (13)	84
Dean Saunders (13)	84
Stephanie Dutton (14)	85
Zoe Thaxter (14)	85
Dean Stone (13)	85
Ashleigh Gaynor (13)	86
Emma Martin (12)	86
Scott Mitchell (13)	86
Gisele Nishimwe (13)	87
Tommy Prescott (13)	87
Louise Larter (13)	87
Seher Bellikli (11)	88
Tiffany Mok (11)	88
Chloe Miller (12)	88
Danielle Jade Davies (13)	89
Charlie Gummer (13)	89
Claire Hossack (11)	89
Caroline Stakalls (13)	90
Emma Marlow (12)	90
Natasha Hall (14)	90
Haydon Godbeer (12)	91
Natalie Morisse (12)	91
Holly Simmons (12)	91

Haling Manor High School
    Wafa Hussein (13)   92

Pyrford Centre
    George McConnachie (15)   93
    Shane Cummins (15)   94

Sutton High School
    Hannah Tiernan (12)   94
    Katrina Watson (14)   95
    Alexandra Sadler (12)   95
    Lucy Rhiannon Penwarden (15)   96
    Elizabeth Yentumi (12)   97
    Sophie Kavanagh (12)   98
    Lucy Yaqub (12)   99
    Indresh Umaichelvam (14)   100
    Meghan Tomacki (15)   100
    Sheryl Ann Odame (11)   101
    Amy Rosier (11)   101
    Charlotte Trefusis (11)   102
    Grishma Shanbhag (13)   102
    Emma Dee (11)   103
    Cara Marguerite Hyde (11)   104
    Annabel Reed (15)   105
    Nicola Hensley (11)   106
    Shruti Jhalla (12)   106
    Maria Pierides (16)   107
    Charlotte Irvine (12)   107
    Niresha Umaichelvam (11)   108
    Lauren Williamson (12)   108
    Sophie Dix (12)   109
    Lara Battinson (12)   109
    Harriet Hewett (14)   110
    Helen Thorpe (15)   111
    Hannah Patrick (12)   112
    Maisie James (12)   112
    Karina Siba (14)   113
    Catherine Branter (12)   113
    Emma Inkester & Sarah Infante (16)   114
    Harriet Trefusis (13)   115

Keerthana Nimaleswaran (12)	115
Holly Ramsey (12)	116
Lucinda Maria Vieira Martins (12)	117
Victoria Hallam (13)	118
Elise Dalman (12)	119
Laura Hamer (13)	120
Sarah Willis (14)	121
Camilla Barden (12)	122
Stephanie Yook (14)	122
Shaline Fazal (13)	123
Taler Kelly (11)	123
Niamh Connaughton (13)	124
Esther Nicoll (14)	125
Elizabeth Main-Ian (12)	126
Tharani Packiahrajah (11)	126
Charlotte Howson (13)	127
Fleur Godwin (11)	127
Sonia Tong (12)	128
Priyanka Amin (13)	129
Karis Kennedy (12)	130
Fiona Cooper (13)	131
Santina Philips (14)	132
Hasret Sayan (11)	133
Sana Sheikh (13)	134
Poh-Yee Wan (12)	135
Hannah Nicoll (14)	136
Krupa H Thakker (12)	137
Sophie Penwarden (12)	137
Hannah Wastnidge (11)	138
Kathryn Griffiths (14)	139
Carla Busso (13)	140
Josie Rawes (13)	141
Sarah Bishop (11)	142
Laura Gillhespy (11)	143
Jessica Crowson (12)	144
Asha Pankhania (12)	144
Natasha Patel (11)	145
Daisy Ukoko-Rongione (12)	145
Sarah Daoud (12)	146
Kimberley Bennett (11)	147
Jennifer Ferguson (12)	148
Elizabeth Priestley (11)	149

Siân-Louise Tangney (12)	150
Natasha Batish (12)	151
Kyndra Vorster (12)	152
Elizabeth Egbe (12)	153
Sarah Monger-Godfrey (12)	154

The Park School

Shaun Allen (11)	154
Harry Milner (11)	155
Luke Comley (13)	155
The Class of 8H	156
Connor Hobbs (11)	157
Luke Collier (13)	158

Wallington County Grammar School

Ryan Daily (11)	158
Ishan de Silva (11)	159
Josh Beer (12)	160
Christopher Mann (11)	161
Aravind Mootien (11)	162
Harry Pike (11)	162
Robert Maguire (11)	163
George Tully (12)	163
Tom Kindler (12)	164
Edward Stedman (11)	165
Andrew Walsh (12)	166
Luke Davis (11)	167
Michael Giblin-Burnham (12)	168
Lewis Chaplin (12)	168
Thomas Lines (12)	169
Simon Preston (11)	169
Adam Taylor (11)	170
Joe Henderson (11)	171
Daniel Heffernan (11)	172
Calum Gordon (11)	172
James Brignull (11)	173
Ben McLellan (11)	173
Patrick Chea (11)	174
Calum George (11)	175
Rishi Bakrania (11)	176
Adam Lyons (11)	176

Joseph Williamson (11)	177
Shatik Patel (11)	177
Ben Donelien (11)	178
Stuart Eldridge (11)	178
Kwaku Dapaah-Danquah (11)	179
Adam Cousins (12)	179
Timothy McKavanagh (11)	180
Edward Butler (11)	181
Adib Chowdhury (11)	182
Samuel Chislett (11)	183
Shane Freemantle (11)	184
Daniel Heronneau (11)	184
Adam Gye (12)	185
Adam Makumbi (12)	185
Nihar Majmudar (11)	186
Thomas Wainford (12)	187
Ciaran Alli (11)	188
Thomas Housden (11)	188
Benjamin Richardson (11)	189
Christopher Jackson (12)	189
Joshua Bell (11)	190
Jonathan Ganz (11)	191
Michael Peter Brockman (11)	192
Gabriel Nicklin (11)	193
Sam Christy (11)	194
Jaabir Bhogadia (11)	194
Tahir Shivji (11)	195
Anthony Daniel (11)	195
Ahmed Suleman (11)	196
Nandu Sanilkumar (11)	197
Harry Wrightson (12)	198
Ghalib Zaidi (12)	199
John Sing-Key (12)	200
Jonathan Mayo (11)	201
Akil Scafe-Smith (11)	202
Vishnu Jayarajan (11)	203
Matthew Scola (12)	204
Gogulan Karunanithy (12)	205
Muhammad Jaffer (11)	206
Jonathan Evans (11)	207
Laurence Kelly (11)	207
Matthew Bieda (11)	208

Josh Adams (11)	208
Haaris Lone (12)	209
Thomas Tawse (11)	210
Samuel Lewis (11)	211
Joshua Heath (11)	212
Mohammed Kaba (11)	213
Devis Kawuki (11)	214
Andrew James (11)	215
Umar Ghulab	216
Terory Larebo (11)	217
Michael Eglon (12)	218

The Poems

I'll Never Know

Here I am, just all alone
With nowhere to go.
I have no place that I call home,
Nothing of my own.

I've never felt the grass tickling at my feet,
I no longer know the sea,
All I know are dark, long streets,
All I've touched is me.

I cry myself to sleep at nights,
Tomorrow I'll put things right.
I'll pray to see the sun at dawn,
And wake up to a brand new morn.

What did I do to deserve this?
Oh what I'd give for such bliss,
To be hugged, embraced and kissed,
To be told that I've been missed.

So please take me home,
I won't be any trouble,
We'd never ever feel; alone,
We'd be the perfect couple.

You'd ask for nothing in return,
And I'd have naught to give,
We'd always stand strong and firm,
In my heart you'd live.

So now I have you all the way,
I'll never dread another day,
I'll stand up proudly and say
That we'll be together - I pray!

Natasha Dawes (12)
Coombe Girls' School

They're All Fruitcakes

Apple was rushing, see, he was late,
Mango doing the tango, practising for the
Summer fête.
Lemon crying rivers of tears,
Lime trying to overcome his fears.
Coconut promoting his chocolate bar,
Pear playing golf, he's on the 18th par.
Tomato sitting there with a plateful of veg,
Kiwi, banana, strawberry and cherry in a
Fruit bowl on the window ledge.
Grape dancing with his peachy friend,
While pineapple's driving watermelon right
Around the bend.
Oh no, they are all being taken,
I hope not to bake with, maybe it's not too bad
Because they're all fruitcakes!

Natasha Hussey (12)
Coombe Girls' School

See You Again

I may as well have been stabbed in the heart,
Because that's what it feels like now we're apart,
You're the only one who would ever have died for me,
You gave your life to set me free.
You will always be my one true love,
But now you have gone straight up above.
My heart belongs to you, my dear,
I have a reason why I won't shed a tear.
It's because I know you are always near me,
In my heart you will always be.
One day my sunset will set for ever,
Then once again we will be together.
We will dance until the day starts breaking,
And finally my heart will stop aching.

Venice Byatt (13)
Coombe Girls' School

The Lost Kitten

I'm hungry, lost and cold,
my fur is soaking wet,
I'm trying to stay alive and bold,
but the future is looking like death.

I eat very little,
like bones and bits of things,
and my tail is bound up,
by boys with lots of string.

I'm trying to waddle on,
but my paws are covered in mud,
I'm trying to settle down,
but I know my life's a dud.

My eyes are rolling into my head,
my beating heart is slowing,
so I know that soon I will be dead,
and I'm going, going, going!

Reed Thomas-Litman (13)
Coombe Girls' School

Love Or Hate

I love you but I hate you
so which one is it?

Is it I love to hate you
or is it I hate to love you?

Or maybe I love to love you
and hate to hate you?

Or is it that I hate
to write a poem you'll love?

Charlene Edwards (13)
Coombe Girls' School

Make A Noise

Do you play an instrument?
It doesn't matter if you're a lady or gent.
I play the flute,
You can just give your horn a hoot;
What about the trumpet?
Of maybe just give the drum a hit.
All ages can play,
All you have to do is say,
Give the whistle a blow,
It doesn't matter how fast or slow.
Listen to the rhythm and tap, tap, tap,
Do a little rap, rap, rap.
You can dance or sing,
You can do everything.
Listen to the beat,
And tap your feet.
Make your family play,
Make sure you get your own way.
What about the keyboard?
Or just rev up the engine of your Ford.
Bang the saucepans,
And clap your hands.
Play it loud,
Play it proud.
Just make a noise.

Charlotte McVay (13)
Coombe Girls' School

Love Poem

I loved you once,
I love you still,
I always have,
I always will.

You're in my heart
Through night and day,
This is the place
You'll always stay.

Doesn't matter
Where we are,
We love each other,
Near or far.

If we drift
And fall apart,
There'll be a place
Still in my heart.

That is where
You'll always stay,
That special place,
Till my last day.

And that means
Everyone can see
Just how much
You mean to me.

Sarah Fry (14)
Coombe Girls' School

????

I took a knife, very sharp, very pointed,
I inserted it deep, cutting up, cutting down,
Across and side to side,
Moving to the top with great precision,
I cut a jagged edge,
The top I removed with care,
I used the spoon as a scoop,
Removing the inside, it now became hollow,
What I had created
Gave me a hard stare,
Into it I placed a candle,
Took a match and lit it,
There it was complete, my creation,
I turned out the lights and watched it glow,
The face lit up the candle flickering,
Through the eyes, the mouth, the nose,
There was a knock at the door, it was time to go,
For it was *Hallowe'en*.

Amy Green (13)
Coombe Girls' School

9/11

The reason for terrorists is painfully unknown,
'Why?' we ask in despair.
Human lives swept and blown,
Hurtling into towers that memorable day,
Leaves me in a land far, far away,
Haunting us for ever, that memorable day.

These terrorists made the smoke billow through the air,
These terrorists kill innocent people and don't even care,
These terrorists in a split second tear apart normal family lives,
These terrorists cause pain and sadness for the world's
                                    disbelieving eyes,
September 11th burns in the backs of our minds.

Katie Proudlove (12)
Coombe Girls' School

Freddy And Ki-Ki

Ki-Ki the bunny lived in a hole
In there lived Freddy the mole.
Freddy and Ki-Ki were the best of friends,
When suddenly one day their friendship did end,
Freddy moved far, far away,
In a land called Mole Hay.
Ki-Ki missed him very much,
But promised that she'd keep in touch.
She wrote to him every day,
So many things she had to say.
Then, one day, Freddy came back,
With lots of presents in a sack.
They hugged and cried,
And Ki-Ki sighed,
They promised their friendship would always last,
And that their problems were all in the past.

Sarah Eastop (12)
Coombe Girls' School

Hallowe'en

Trick or treat, trick or treat,
may we have something to eat?
Spiders, bats and pumpkins too,
witches stirring up their brew.
The werewolf howls, the full moon's out,
black cats lurking out and about.
Shadows whisper in the dark,
who dares enter the empty park?
The haunted sky is black and clear,
listen to the sounds you hear.
it's the time of the year when nothing's the same,
and no one seems quite so tame,
so watch which corner that you take
because it may be a mistake.

Abby Keaveney (13)
Coombe Girls' School

The Womb

My delicate little fingers,
My delicate little toes,
My big, delicate body,
My tiny, little nose.

I lift up my heavy head,
And I'll come out soon
Just like Mum said.

Looking up and looking down,
First I smile and then I frown,
Stretch out straight and then I'm curled.

So now I realise I'm in my own little world.

Months, weeks and days have passed.
I'm sailing a ship but with no mast,
I kick, kick and kick even more
Until I get past the closed, locked door.

Pinching and punching until I get out,
I'll get out safely, you'll see, no doubt.

Emily Britton (13)
Coombe Girls' School

Spring

The flowers,
The lambs,
Now spring is here.

The birds sing,
The showers,
Now spring is here.

Now spring is here,
Now spring is here,
Now spring is here.

Rosalie Vanderpant (12)
Coombe Girls' School

Dear Diary

Daddy hit me again today,
And Mum, well she went away,
How I hope, how I hope
That I'll learn how to cope
With Daddy's so very strange ways.

Some strange people came round today,
And then they took Daddy away,
How I pray, how I pray
That I'm taken away
From my foster mum's threatening ways.

The strange people took me back today,
My foster mum, she didn't get away,
How I dream, how I dream
They can make up a scheme
To get me to my real mum and her ways.

Mummy hit me again today,
And Dad? He got locked away,
How I hope, how I hope
That I learn how to cope
With Mummy's so very sad ways.

Flynn Thomas-Litman (12)
Coombe Girls' School

Emotions

The sun was smiling,
The sea was shining,
The moon was sleepy,
The clouds were weepy.

The trees were dreary,
The lakes were weary,
The birds were pleased,
And the world was at ease.

Laura Sowell (12)
Coombe Girls' School

Like An Eagle

Like an eagle I was born to fly
Right across the open sky,
Without you I couldn't see
Because you and me are meant to be.

Like an eagle I was born to fly
And to you I'd never lie,
When I'm with you I can't breathe,
I never want you to leave.

Like an eagle I was born to fly
In the sky, way up high,
I love you and I am true,
Please tell me that you love me too.

Like an eagle I was born to trust,
Trust the man I've come to love,
So take my hand and fly with me,
Come fly through the midnight sky with me.

Elekia Akhuetie (12)
Coombe Girls' School

The War Of Mankind

Cannons blazing,
Guns smoking,
Women running,
Arms flailing.

Tanks bring men
Into town
To start the war
Of all mankind.

Fathers and brothers
Go to fight,
But will we see
Our men return?

Tessa Tyler Todd (12)
Coombe Girls' School

Seen Through The Eyes Of A River

When I was born I became a spring,
Then a stream that flowed down the mountains,
I saw lots of things I'd never seen before,
Like fishes with golden scales and grassy meadows.

Animals drank from my smooth, silky skin,
The sun glowed on me and flickers of light danced on my surface.

When I became a river, I turned and twisted,
The meanders were like a roller coaster,
It was such an adventure.

At the end, when I was getting old,
People threw their rubbish in me like
I was their trash can,
I wondered what I had done to deserve this.

Rashel Rassapour (12)
Coombe Girls' School

I Have An Idea

I have an idea for the world to be one,
I have an idea that's only just begun,
It whirls round in my head night and day,
It's just a vision I see my way!

I have an idea of the world as a better place,
A place of love, care, happiness and grace.
No more war and no more greed,
A place with not a single bad deed!

I have an idea of children never to be scared,
I have an idea for them to be loved and cared.
It doesn't matter what colour, race, religion you are,
Let yourself free, you're not behind a bar!

I believe this strongly and I'll tell you why I do,
It's because I believe in people that live in this world,
Just as I believe my idea will come *true!*

Antoaneta Roussinova (13)
Coombe Girls' School

Hallowe'en Poem

The 30th October is when it all began,
'Trick or treat' is what the kids sang.
The full moon's out in the clear, black sky,
And all around the witches fly.

Devils with their shiny, red horns,
Tails sharp as thin brown thorns,
Pumpkins gleaming with tons of light,
Showing their faces in the night.

Frogs' legs, cats' tails, dogs' teeth too,
Mix around in the witches' brew.
Vampires' teeth, blood dripping,
Witches cause high-pitched screeching.

Ghosts in sheets, all are white,
Kids scream at this sight.
Midnight's when the ghouls and spectres depart,
Hoping for next year to start.

Jessica Archard (13)
Coombe Girls' School

Spring

When spring arrives,
The bright sun rises,
The flowers open their eyes
To find themselves a wonderful surprise!

The flowers sway from side to side,
The fresh breeze blows at them with pride,
The clear river glistens under the sun,
Everyone loves spring, you have so much fun!

As the sun starts to settle,
It burns bright red,
The moon rises up to the sky,
And the sun goes to bed.

Emily Powell (12)
Coombe Girls' School

Rainy Afternoon

I sit there by the windowpane,
Watching as it heavily rains.
The clouds look a dark shade of grey,
I feel it's a miserable day.

As I turn and look around,
I see no squirrels scampering on the ground,
Everything is quiet, I hear no noise,
As the rain falls silently onto the ground.

Nothing is moving, everything is still,
The wind is stronger than ten windmills,
I just sit there hungry, disappointed and bored,
I listen as the fierce wind roars.

The time is now ticking away,
In the spring days of cold May,
Dissatisfied and bored, I just sit there,
Without thinking, I just sit and stare.

Where is the sun? I stare and seek,
The weather today is too bleak,
I want to go outside and play,
I hope the rain will go away.

Now the rain is spitting lightly,
And the sun is shining slightly,
The blazing sun is shining over me,
The scorching sun is shining brightly,
Today is a wonderful day.

     Hooray!

Aiswarya Sivagnanam (13)
Coombe Girls' School

Spring Has Sprung!

April is here with its gentle showers,
Soaking to the roots of plants and flowers,
Easing the drought of March away,
The climbing sun extends each day,
Warming and lighting the darkness of Earth,
So many leaves and buds are given birth.

March gales give way to gentle breeze,
As newborn birds sing in the trees.
Animals awake from deep winter sleep,
With joy and pleasure, lambs and rabbits leap.
Children look for fairy gold
At ends of rainbows as stories are told.

The day is older, soon it is dark night,
All becomes calm, and what a pretty sight.
In black, velvet sky floats silvery moon,
Sailing and drifting like a child's balloon.
Moving clouds let bright stars appear,
As the night sky begins to clear.

Spring has sprung.

Hatice Resa (12)
Coombe Girls' School

Wimbledon Tennis

My week of tennis starts
with an ace!
At the end of the day it
has become a race!
Every day there is a fresh
new lawn!
We must finish quickly before
we get caught in the storm!

Lizzie Foulds (12)
Coombe Girls' School

The Giant Seeks Revenge

The men have invaded his world,
The boat appears black and skeletal against the snowy landscape,
The boat means warmth, shelter, a home.
The giant seeks revenge,
The ice can kill the boat.
The giant orders the snow to strangle the boat.

The boat is heaved upwards like a toy,
The rigging appears like strings
Of broken instruments,
Crushing makes these strings sag,
Like spiders' webs.
The giant seeks revenge.

Snow is blown onto the ropes,
Icicles shiver down onto the deck,
Sails tear like paper,
As the boat is squeezed.
Beams break,
The boat suffocates,
Life is screwed and crushed
Out of the boat.
The men are homeless.
The giant gets his revenge.

Kayantha Sivalingam (12)
Coombe Girls' School

Auntie

Every time I dream, I see her face,
Every time I sleep, she's in my mind,
Every time I close my eyes, I see her grace,
Every time I picture her, she was so kind.
Every time I think of her,
She will always be on my mind.

Emma Weston (12)
Coombe Girls' School

Night Nightmares

Wolves howling like the breeze,
Wind freezing my knees,
Walking, walking,
Round, up and down.

Stumble through the broken gate,
Looking, thinking, *what is my fate?*
Walking, walking,
Round, up and down.

Door closed, as cobwebs cover,
Finding people, is there another?
Walking, walking,
Round, up and down.

Down the stairs, up others,
Wanting to hide under my duvet covers,
Walking, walking,
Round, up and down.

Movements stir within the shadow,
Making no noise as I go.

Walking, walking,
Round, up and *stop!*

Kirstyn Luton (12)
Coombe Girls' School

Poppy

Have you ever wondered
About the men and women too
Who put their lives forward
To save me and you.

Leaving behind their friends and family,
Defending and fighting for our lives.
To watch gunshots and death
Before their very eyes.

Have you ever wondered
How they feel now?
Battered, scarred and wounded,
I can't imagine how.

But as I watch the TV screen,
And see them marching, frail but proud,
Medals gleaming in the morning sun,
The bugle playing its mournful song and the cannon fires, oh so loud.

Have you ever wondered
About the poppy on your chest?
It symbolizes those brave, loyal soldiers.
They simply are the best.

Sophie Croft (11)
Coombe Girls' School

Längflue

The mountains are green with snow-white hair,
Rocks reach up like a proud nose in the air,
Deep paths lie within like the marks from a scowl,
Ridges of forest curve away like brows.

Does the ice creak like the sound of ancient bones,
And the trickle of a spring seem like blood from a wound?
At the whooshing of our skis does it flick back its hair,
Or does it just do it to give us a scare?

How does it feel as jet planes scream overhead,
Or a thousand climbers' boots vibrate, tread over tread?
How does it feel with mountain huts upon your shoulders,
And cable cars, crawling like spiders, full of pass holders?

For millions of years you remained undisturbed,
But now are a playground of a huge human herd.
For millions of years you will always be there
For you are one of the Alps.

Laura Burrows (11)
Coombe Girls' School

My Best Friend!

My best friend is there,
she is everywhere.
I've known her since I was young,
we are two of a kind.

She is very fair,
an independent girl.
She has her own style
and she is rare.

She has determination,
doing what she does.
She's the best and that's why,
she's my best friend.

Xoana Rodriguez (11)
Coombe Girls' School

No One Noticed

She always sits alone in the corner
It is like she is invisible
Everyone just ignores her
She is always laughed at
No one will notice when she is gone.

She looks in the mirror and cries
She sees all her imperfections
She wishes she could do something right
She is lost and she feels all alone
No one will notice when she is gone

Her head hurts from confusion
She is weak and has had enough
Her spirit is broken from the pain
Her shoulders carry heavy boulders
No one will notice when she is gone

She wants to escape and be free
She sees death as a way of leaving Hell
She looks to God and prays for help
Her prayers are pleas for help and freedom
No one will notice when she is gone

One day she was there, the next she was gone
People didn't notice she was gone
A policeman asked them about her death
Then they realised what they had done
No one noticed when she was gone

They wished they had just said, 'Hi.'
Ignoring her had killed her
No one could imagine her pain
More importantly no one tried
No one noticed she was gone.

Shareen Hearn (13)
Coombe Girls' School

Can You?

Can you hear the last words of a dying soldier?
Can you see the bloody wound in his stomach?
Can you smell the smoke from the gun?

Can you hear the cries of a widow?
Can you see the tears on her face?
Can you smell the smoke of her candle?

Can you hear the sob of a child?
Can you see the photo of his lost one?
Can you smell the dinner he has not eaten?
Can you touch his cold, wet face?

Do you have the senses of a victim?
Don't make war your fate.

Francesca Jacques (12)
Coombe Girls' School

World War . . . ?

Bang, bang, bang.

Bang, bang, here,
Bang, bang, there,
Bang, bang, everywhere.

People dying here,
People dying there,
People dying everywhere.

Everyone crying here,
Everyone crying there,
Everyone crying everywhere.

Bang, bang, here,
Bang, bang, there,
Bang, bang, everywhere.

Bang, bang, bang . . .

Apoorva Khosti (12)
Coombe Girls' School

Little Boy

A pain in the back, that little boy,
All he does is play with that stupid toy,
Watches TV all day and doesn't care what anyone says,
His brain is hard to understand, just like a maze.

But he is still little and cute,
Sometimes I wish I had a control for him and I could just press mute,
He is quite fun and we do have a laugh when we play,
He is nicest in the sweet month of May.

This is a description of my brother,
While I think about it, I wouldn't replace him for another,
The person who always pulls my hair,
The brother who really does care.

Georgina Edwards (11)
Coombe Girls' School

Rest In Peace

One moment you're here,
The next you're gone,
But you're still in my heart,
And hearts do go on.
Every day I imagine what life would be
If you were living here with me.

I try so hard to picture that day,
When we meet again,
Every night I pray.
One day we will,
I'm sure of that,
I love you for ever my brother, I do,
Stick with me
And I'll stick with you.

Jahdine Milosevic (13)
Coombe Girls' School

Friends

When I'm feeling down,
My friends will be around.
We go out every day
To hang around and play.

Together in school,
Meeting in the swimming pool.
How I admire my friends,
Friends till the end!

Sometimes arguments appear,
Usually we're all in tears.
Then I lose my friends,
But soon enough it ends!

My friends are always there,
Friends who really care.
How will I get from day to day without my friends?
When in need of help, they always lend.

Ella Edey (11)
Coombe Girls' School

Autumn's Here

Summer days come and go
And autumn days came not too long ago
And see the leaves falling,
Now the autumn days are calling.
See the orange, yellow and brown colours
Scattered all around,
The autumn mist has filled the air,
With autumn colours everywhere!

Hana Al-Amiri (13)
Coombe Girls' School

My Parents

They are always there for me,
They never let me down,
I love them very much,
Even though my dad always acts like a clown.

We have been everywhere together,
France, Spain, Denmark, America and even the Caribbean,
Whenever I'm feeling really sad,
They tell me over and over again, 'Cheer up, everything's not so bad.'

They can embarrass me, humiliate me and make me wish the
                                        ground would just swallow me up,
At times they make me want to shout, kick, scream and much more,
However, when all I want to do is shut myself in my room,
They somehow always get me wishing that I never hated them.

But don't you think that if parents didn't do that, life would seem
                                                        very empty?

Anna Driscoll (11)
Coombe Girls' School

Seasons

Spring

Spring is the time of year when flowers start to bloom,
Spring is the time of year when we emerge from the gloom.

Summer

Summer is the time of year when people come out and have fun,
Summer is the time of year when we all lie around in the sun.

Autumn

Autumn is the time of year when leaves turn and fall,
Autumn is the time of year when the trees don't look so tall.

Winter

Winter is the time of year when days start to get shorter,
Winter is the time of year when the weather starts to get colder.

Tessa Lloyd (11)
Coombe Girls' School

Dream

(This poem is called Dream because happiness is a dream to me. To me dreams seem to be just that . . . dreams.)

Don't look at me,
You don't know,
The girl that is inside of me.

Don't try and catch
My attention.
I don't want you to know.

I said leave me alone
Where I can hear my soul,
Burning with rage and envy.

You don't know me
And you never will.
You don't know
What goes on in my mind.

My feelings don't matter to you,
I can't confide in you,
You don't understand what I think and feel,
It's all a foreign language to you.

Why is life so complicated?
With hate and fear in everyone's eyes.
Tears that never stop running
Down children's rosy cheeks.

I dream of life filled with happiness
Where sadness is banished back to a story in wonderland
And smiles replace terror and anger.
But then I realise that is all it is . . .

A dream.

Sian Macarty Cole (12)
Coombe Girls' School

I Admire . . .

I admire Arsenal
For getting all the way to the top,
As they have been through quite a lot.

Arsenal are my favourite team,
They're red not purple, blue or green.

They have become unbeatable this season,
But I like them not for this reason,
Even if they went to the bottom,
To me, they will never be forgotten.

I will follow them all the way,
Right to that very day
When the team starts to break away!

One day I would like to meet them,
Or even go and watch them play,
And hopefully that will come true one very special day!

Amelia Bradley (12)
Coombe Girls' School

Beware, Beware

Green eyes with their mysterious stare,
This black cat is sure to scare.
Black wings, sharp fangs,
Upside down the bat hangs.
Claws for toes, no ears or a nose,
This vicious owl sits in his stony pose.

The chilling sound of night-time howling,
These predatory wolves are slinking and prowling.
This eight-legged creature will give a bad bite,
This spider's crawling will give you a fright.
There's nothing there but you sense a stare,
This ghost makes you think there's nobody there.

Stay inside *beware, beware,*
Hallowe'en is a frightful scare!

Claudia Adolphus (11)
Coombe Girls' School

Exams

Thump, thump, thump!
I can feel my heart pump!
'Silence!' Shouts the teacher
To us she's just a fierce creature.
90 minutes on the clock,
Tick-tock, tick-tock.

Students in front and behind
All tables neatly in a line.
Stuck in a hall
With girls, big and small.
60 minutes on the clock,
Tick-tock, tick-tock.

Concentration is essential
And keeping cool is fundamental.
Everyone else is writing so fast,
What if I'm one of the last?
15 minutes on the clock
Tick-tock, tick-tock, tick-tock.

Panic! Mental block
Fingers locked.
5 seconds on the clock
Tick-tock, tick-tock.

Pencils down
everyone *stop!*
Tick-tock, tick-tock.

Kiran Bejawn (12)
Coombe Girls' School

Gramp, Champ!
(RIP 4/01/1943-28/05/2004)

Fun, fantastic, fascinating, fearless.
He taught me so much,
Though I never felt his touch;
I've been told of his kindness,
And how he's happy regardless;
'Larger than life,'
Say his kids and wife.

Terrific, tremendous, talented, towering tall.
Nigeria is where he lived,
And how he was happy to love and to give;
Six houses is how many he bought,
I'll leave it to my kids, he thought;
He left his mark on Earth,
Everyone loved him between death and birth.

Great, gifted, giving, gone.
Heaven is his home now,
Remembering him is my vow;
Father, husband, property investor, engineer,
With all these jobs he was in top gear;
I always knew he was the best,
And now he lies in peace to rest!

Chanel Cullen (12)
Coombe Girls' School

The Jolly Boy Next Door

The jolly boy next door was a happy lad,
Always playing and never sad.

Then one day there was a knock at the door,
Come on soldier you're off to war.

Into the trenches, they all jumped in,
To fight the battle they hoped to win.

All that was heard was bombs and shots,
They were still rather an encouragable lot.

As time went on they couldn't take much more,
Slaughter and murder that's what they saw.

He'd had no contact with his family, there was no phone,
So the jolly boy next door staggered home.

But the jolly boy next door,
Was jolly no more.

Emma Brown (12)
Coombe Girls' School

War And Hate

Is war because people don't get along?
Is war because people don't know where they belong?
Is war because people don't know right from wrong?
War is because of people.

Is there hate because people don't get on with each other?
Is there hate because people don't listen to their father or mother?
Is there hate because people should be free, then run for cover?
War is because of people.

Beryl Kumpha (12)
Coombe Girls' School

The Life Of A Daffodil

I wake up at the beginning of the day,
Opening my petals out all the way.
Ahh! The lovely sun warming me up from yesterday's breeze
Oh I really did freeze.

Oh no what's that, I hear a bee,
Coming here right towards me.
Oh no! Oh no! What shall I do?
My nectar shall be gone too!

He's coming closer, closer and near,
I have everything to fear.
Hey what's that he has become invisible,
I don't care at least I'm still visible.

Maybe he's gone far away,
Far away to another place.
Now it's night, I can rest,
Hopefully tomorrow the bee won't be a pest.

Bijal Bhundia (12)
Coombe Girls' School

Trick Or Treat - If You Dare

Holding onto someone's arm as you creep to the door,
Jumping at the sound of a scream from the moor.
Shouting, 'Trick or treat!' and then running away,
Now that's the only game to play.
Witches on broomsticks fly past you and they cackle in delight,
Silhouettes of cats run past you in the moonlight.
Ears pricking up, at the terrifying sound of whom?
'Over by the woods,' she said and then silence before the full moon.
I don't think you'll forget this Hallowe'en!

Georgia Sergant (11)
Coombe Girls' School

Cold Feet

I hate to have a cold foot or toe,
So I always wear a pair of socks,
I don't always wear socks that go,
But I keep them all in a large box.

One night when in bed,
A sock fell off,
I thought my foot was dead
And the coldness made me cough.

So I searched my whole room,
I searched every nook and cranny,
I even used a broom
And I looked like my granny.

After searching the whole house,
I knew where it must be
And then curling up like a mouse,
I wished I were a tree.

For the sock was in the most dangerous place,
A place that makes you screw up your face,
A place where you cannot really see,
A place where there is not one shout of glee.

In this place you probably already know,
You must use a torch to give you a glow,
The place is under the bed where the darkness dawns on you
And you must be prepared for a monster shouting, *'Boo!'*

In fact, in this place, you must be prepared for anything,
For a loud bang, crash, clang or ding,
But now it's all over, and I have my sock, yay!
And this is how it happened by the way:

I looked under the bed,
All armoured up,
But nothing banged me on the head,
And nothing made a loud noise except my *hiccup*.

I grabbed my sock and then jumped onto the bed,
I'd seen a ghost that looked like an ape
And I saw another head,
It was dark and absurd and rather out of shape.

So even though I'd collected that sock,
I will always be afraid of under the bed,
The place where you can hear a tick-tock
And the place where everything's dead!

Sarah Dyson (12)
Coombe Girls' School

The Spicy Pepper

I ate a spicy pepper,
For a joke made at a fair,
The pepper seized my scalp on fire,
And burnt off all my hair.

Gallons of water gushed out my eyes,
And steam fired out my nose,
A red-hot flame burned in my mouth,
As I ran in search of a hose.

I bolted around the house
And jumped to touch the ceiling.
For the fan stuck upon it,
Could relieve my painful feeling.

I dashed into the kitchen,
In search of any ice,
I swung the fridge door open,
But all I saw was rice.

Over time, my hair grew back again
And the fire turned to smoke,
But I've learnt my lesson now,
It was only for a joke!

Morsal Sherzad (13)
Coombe Girls' School

Writer's Block

Writer's block's the worst,
When you just can't get inspired.
Your ideas seem to come to a halt,
You're feeling much too tired.

Your brain just will not think,
You try to knock it into gear.
There's nothing to get you back on track,
That blank space is easy to fear.

You want to write something exciting,
Something fast and flowing,
Something deep and meaningful,
Something that gets you going.

You can't think of rhyming words
Writer's block's the worst,
Something comes to mind and then,
You just can't finish the verse.

Then again all writers get it,
It's something very common.
It's a pain in the p'touie,
It makes you feel quite solemn.

Everything you seem to write,
It all just gets erased
And then your mind won't work again,
It's a problem that must be faced.

Then a strange thing happens,
When I go to bed,
The words they seem to jump at me,
And won't go out of my head!

Emily Patton (12)
Coombe Girls' School

Boys!

Sophie and me are best of friends,
We love boys, well especially Mends.
Mends is a boy that drives me mad,
And I am his girlfriend that makes me glad!

Sophie and me are best of friends,
Sophie loves Steven, we're always down his ends.
We call him 'A' boy because of his top,
And he looks really buff when he tries to bop.

Sophie and me are best of friends,
We love boys that write their tags in fat pens.
We would never talk to boys that graff in mustard yellow,
Otherwise we will never say hello.

Sophie and me are best of friends,
We really like a boy called Kens,
He cheated one of us so he was out the door,
He came back so we threw him on the floor.

Amy Lawrence (12)
Coombe Girls' School

Christmas

C elebrations for everybody having fun
H olidays with your family, your dad and your mum
R oast dinners and families around the table
I want my name to be on every present's label.
S tars twinkling nrightly in the sky
T hinking what, with all my new money, to buy
M aking Christmas plays and carol singing
A mazing dreams of what Santa will be bringing
S tockings filled with presents, Christmas is coming!

Jennie Murchie (13)
Coombe Girls' School

Changes In The World

The people have changed some way, somehow
And the people act different by racism
Every day people looked at differently now
The world is destroyed by hate.

There's less love in the world than there was before
Some do anything just to get their hands on money
Instead people love this paper more and more
Something's wrong with the world, this is serious, not funny!

People take drugs and drink alcohol
They'd do anything just to get their hands on it
They start to lose their minds and lose control
After a while they will find it hard to quit!

All this fuss and fighting between the countries
Can't we get along for at least one day?
It's been going on for many centuries
We act like animals fighting for prey!

The world has to end someday
So make the world a better place
Have a good time and enjoy your stay
Just smile at every different face!

Zena Daniel (13)
Coombe Girls' School

Life Is What It Is . . .

Life is a ride
And you've got a ticket,
So when you find a pencil,
Go on and flick it.
Life's meant for living,
So go on and live it,
Like a ball's meant for kicking,
So go on and kick it.

Life is a roller coaster
And you have to ride it,
So when your shoe is scuffed,
Go on and shine it.
A kite's meant for flying,
So go on and fly it,
Life's a plain white canvas,
So go on and dye it!

Life's what it is
And I'm gonna live it,
Make the most of what I have
And give it all I can give it.

Shaista Kerai (11)
Coombe Girls' School

War

Trudge, trudge, trudge, trudge,
Rode the British in the cold.

Trudge, trudge, trudge, trudge,
Into battle they were told.

They stepped into battle on the front line,
Victory was theirs it was just a matter of time.

Some wished for baths,
The ones covered in dirt.

Others wished for bandages,
The ones that were hurt.

Some nearly killed themselves,
They couldn't take much more,

Slaughter and murder that was
What they saw,

Shots and bombs flying past,
Now that made their hearts beat very fast.

'We've won!' They heard someone shout,
But some sat full of doubt.

Trudge, trudge, trudge, trudge,
Rode the British in the cold.
Trudge, trudge, trudge, trudge,
To their family they were told.

Lucy Brown (12)
Coombe Girls' School

Confession

It was love at first sight
Do you know I see you every morning
When you walk past me.

You took all my heart
You took my soul
I want to give all my love
I want to give everything I have
I want to show you that I love you.

I want to be brave and strong
To tell you that I love you but
I'm too afraid to tell.
I hate myself every time when I see
Myself in the mirror,
That I'm too weak.

I'd rather hurt myself and
Finish my love.

Nevertheless, before I finish my love
I'm going to confess to you
That I love you,
    I love you . . .

Jeong-Inn Kim (13)
Coombe Girls' chool

Running For Your Team

Kelly Holmes sweating with fear
Listen to the crowd, hear them cheer
Running for Britain
The Olympics is near
Practise, practise
For runner of the year

Her nerves are roaring
The cheering of her friends
The schoolgirl's running
Running to reach the end
Thoughts of her idol coming into her head
Her heart is pounding, she's losing her breath
She is nearly there, nearly at the end
'Come on you can do it!' says the voice inside her head

The England flag on the back of her shirt
The pressure's on her so is achievement and dirt
She can't help thinking of her proud, young fans
Watching her on the telly all over the land
Cheering her name and hoping, hoping
Whispering, 'Come on Kelly, you can do it, you can win.'

Poppy Newman (11)
Coombe Girls' School

Shark Atta . . .

We were drifting about in the water,
On the wide open sea,
We were floating about with the flotsam,
Myself, Max, Laura and Lee.

Ripples distracted my thoughts,
A large grey fin appeared,
I tried to swim over to Laura,
Hello, has Max disappeared?

We were sure it would come back for more,
So I started to swim towards Lee,
I shouldn't have left poor old Laura,
Because now there was just him and me.

The shark was swiftly returning,
I lamented, 'Let it eat me!'
It must have heard my crying,
As it turned and went for Lee!

Looking around for an island,
Was that a mirage or sand?
Just swim a little faster,
I'm almost on dry la . . .

Emily Finch (11)
Coombe Girls' School

My Dream

One night, I dreamt of a peaceful garden,
The next night, I dreamt of a beautiful garden.
The third night, they were gone -
Gone somewhere where nobody will ever find.

A few days later, I dreamt of the ruins of my peaceful garden,
The next night, my beautiful garden was destroyed.
The third night, I dreamt of nothing, nothing at all -
Will I ever find my garden again?

My peaceful garden was ruined,
My beautiful garden was destroyed,
Who would do such a thing?

My peaceful garden must have left me,
Left me all alone,
Now I understand,
I have left my friends all alone,
I have learnt my lesson,
I won't leave them again.

My beautiful garden must have left me,
Left me and hurt my feelings,
Now I understand,
I have said nasty things and hurt their feelings,
I have learnt my lesson,
I won't hurt their feelings again.

I have learnt all my lessons,
Will my gardens come back?
Will my nightmares go?

Yeah-Been Suh (12)
Coombe Girls' School

The Darkness

It's coming, it's coming,
It's creeping through bushes,
Like a tiger hunting his prey.

It's getting nearer and nearer,
As my world seems to be flying away,
Like galloping horses.

It's getting faster and faster,
Roaming wherever it likes,
Like a horse with no rider.

It's found me, it's found me,
There's nowhere to hide, it has me,
Like a lion and a mouse.

Nothing, nothing,
I sit there waiting, waiting for the worst,
Like someone about to be found guilty.

It's going, it's going,
It's slowly creeping away,
Like a tortoise in a race.

It's gone, it's gone,
My fears have gone today,
Like a shooting star took them all away.

The light, the light,
Because the dark has gone,
Like the sun on a rainy day.

Rosina Martin (12)
Coombe Girls' School

The Message

I am writing from what is in my heart,
To tell my friends and family, that we are not far apart.

Even if you live half-way across the world,
The friendship and love we share will always be held.

Your heart chooses who it likes and who it does not,
At least five people will die for you, have you ever given that
A thought?

You have helped me and now I shall help you,
What I speak is from my heart and true.

If it wasn't for my friends and family I would not be the person
I am today,
I guess the most important things are the hardest to say.

Just before I end and write the message I have to say,
These are the things I thought of at the end of the day.

I have sent out the ring of love,
This very ring is carried by a dove,
The love is shared and will reach all,
For this dove shall never fail or fall.

Message: Don't be afraid to tell someone that you love them.
Reach out and tell someone what they mean to you,
Because when you decide to, it may be too late.
Seize the day,
Never have any regrets.

Remember: love is priceless.

Nan Pancoast (12)
Coombe Girls' School

My Ocean Imagination

I will fill my ocean imaginations,
with the clearest and bluest water,
fresh from a clear, turquoise river.

The sound of the roaring blue ocean,
and the echo of silky dolphins singing.

I will collect every raindrop that,
falls from the opaque blanket.

I will wipe the drops that fall
and roll down my cheeks,
like droplet crystals revolving
on the crisp sand.

I can feel the sun rays that hit
on the shored seashells that shimmer
with a chest full of pearls.

The chattering of the misty clams,
that vibrate through the glimmers
of clear liquid.

The winds and waves that blow
all the ocean's scent through
and out the scales of starfish.

An ocean that spreads right out to the sun,
like silk, swaying on the reflection of the stars.

Eujean Cha (12)
Coombe Girls' School

Harmless Fun?

Children knocking on strangers' doors,
In the twilight,
Dressed as ghouls,
Begging for sweets or leaving with threats.
Harmless fun?

Dating back to the Druids of Celtic times,
A festival to worship evil and spirits.
Still around,
But *different, milder.*
Harmless fun?

Pumpkins containing lit candles,
Were believed to guard the home,
Against witches and evil spirits.
Harmless fun?

Costumes in shops, with disgusting faces,
All to make money,
Attract children,
Who want to dress up and knock on strangers' doors.
Harmless fun
Or an excuse to celebrate evil?

Emily Warland (13)
Coombe Girls' School

11th September

A peaceful world, one of dreams exploded in one day
Lives were changed - unrecognisable
No one knew what to say
    The planes crashed
    the towers fell
    and with them loved ones
    a living hell.
Shock, horror, tears, pain
the world will never be the same again
Heroes, countries united in grief
offered very little relief.
A peaceful world no longer
and yet nations, through grief, grew stronger
we children of the future
owe so much to those who died
have to say that we have tried
must remember and make the change
for a better world again.
That awful day we remember
when the world changed on the 11th September
a better place, we have to try
so in vain, they did not die!

Rhian Bamsey (13)
Coombe Girls' School

My Teacher!

My teacher's like no other I've seen,
She wears her old costumes from Hallowe'en.
When reading a book about a magical broom,
She decides to run around the room.

She asks us questions that are always in rhyme,
And she expects the answer in double-quick time.
If we're naughty she locks us in her den,
While wrestling a rubber and silly old pen.

For homework she says that we can't play,
Or watch our TV for the rest of the day.
My teacher's either totally insane,
Or she's a genius with a little brain.

But whether its madness or her teacher powers,
I don't think it matters because I know that she's ours!

Stephanie Tizzard (13)
Coombe Girls' School

Hatred And Peace

Peace
Peace tastes sweet,
Peace feels warm,
Peace is yellow,
Peace sounds like children,
Peace lives in Heaven and Earth.

Hatred
Hatred tastes like a bitter lemon,
Hatred feels like needles poking into you,
Hatred is blood-red,
Hatred sounds like people screaming,
Hatred lives in the depths of Hell.

Peace is what people most desire
And to this is which we must aspire.

Nicole Davies (13)
Coombe Girls' School

Nature Never Lies

The trees so silent, trees so still,
I walk beneath them at my will.
Although the days are so very short,
They will never ever be taught.

Across the river, a ripple proceeds,
A ray of light somewhere be nigh.
I cross the river at steady speed,
To see myself unknown.

Sunrise is coming upon the spring dew.
Daffodils and snowdrops,
Show the colours of their personal hue.

As the night drew into a close,
Snuffly hedgehogs and foxes arose,
With their beady eyes and cunning nose,
The nocturnal animals of the woods doze.

Katherine Adams (12)
Coombe Girls' School

Occasions

Birthdays
On your birthday what do you get?
Chocolate cake, presents, maybe a pet!

Easter
When the Easter bunny comes, hopping in and out,
There will always be some chocolate there, whenever he is about!

Hallowe'en
Hallowe'en is when the kids go out, playing through the night,
But when midnight strikes,
The real things come to give them all a fright!

Christmas
At Christmas we don't want our toys which are old,
We also don't want the weather which is very, very cold!

Alexandra Wright (11)
Coombe Girls' School

Loving, Laughing, Loyal Lavi

I've got a friend called Lavi,
Who's really kind and funny.
She was born on the 19th June,
And she's always over the moon.

She's a really, really fast runner,
She runs at 90 miles per hour.
Lavi has beautiful eyes
And she never ever lies.

Lavi's very loyal and modest,
If you ask her a question, she's honest.
She's as bright as the sun
And a true friend you can rely on

She's very fit and sporty
And isn't at all naughty.
She looks after me so dearly,
She gets into trouble very rarely.

She has very nice hairstyles,
In a race she beats everyone by miles.
She uses lots of Vaseline
And is never ever mean.

She is really good at netball
And has to play people who are extremely tall.
She always has been and always will be a nice friend to me,
That's my poem about loving, laughing, loyal Lavi.

Lindsay Sivakumar (11)
Coombe Girls' School

Forever Into Eternity

Forever into eternity my darling love shall wait.
Wait for me, as I wait for him, our fate will never make a date.
Oh, how I have missed all summer my love.
As perfect memories of the days past,
Our love will never end but always last.
Even though you're not here in my presence,
You remain firmly in my heart.
With your spirit always and forever nearby,
I know we will never part.
I know you're watching down on me from the heavens above.
One thing that shall never change, is that we will always have
                                          a life of love.
Soon enough my time will come,
So forever into eternity, we can be as one.

Candace Grigsby (13)
Coombe Girls' School

Friends

F riends are like flowers; they wilt away and die
    if you don't look after them.
R espect is what you treat your friends with.
I f you want to make more friends you have got
    to be one.
E very friend would want honesty and trust for a
    good friendship.
N o matter what your friend looks like or how they dress,
    a friend is a friend for their personality.
D ifferent people can also be good friends, even if
    you have never known them.
S pecial to you and always there for you,
    that's what real friends do!

Amy House (11)
Coombe Girls' School

Night Mood

The glowing moon rises,
Sizes up the brightest stars,
Like a paper plate,
Soaring towards Mars.

> The burning stars glitter,
> Floating high in the sky,
> Like bits of confetti -
> Like tigers' eyes.

The misty planets hover,
In a ring around the sun,
Like precious jewels,
The night has begun.

> The frosty moon spreads,
> Sweeping shadows everywhere,
> Like a giant blanket,
> A stillness in the air.

The black satin of the still night,
The stars fading away,
A glowing light like embers dying,
The birth of a new day.

Suzie Robson (11)
Coombe Girls' School

Snow

Snowballs falling,
Christmas is calling,
In the season of snow.

Snowflakes falling,
Morning is dawning,
In the season of snow.

Children waking
Breakfast is baking
In the season of snow.

Hats are taken
Children are playing
In the snow.

Although the snow is purely white
Nothing could be dirtier
When everyone has trudged through
So this Christmas remember
That it doesn't happen often
So think . . .

Victoria Bradley (12)
Coombe Girls' School

Fairness

This is my long aired sin.
Everyone's eyes all tell me their dark thoughts
all they want is loving, without any end
all like to explore all sorts by touching and feeling.
Left on their own, they cannot comprehend
in lonely misery how we all try to defend
even just one breath from them.

They lust to have the clarity of freedom,
wanting to use long meditated words.
Their lives are as the fruit of careful acting
stuck in bed with only thoughts and reading,
with endurance, with grace, with wild hearts
even their dreams are lying dappled in the glow of the moonlight,
as they long to learn new, skilful arts.
Why can't we all be fair?
That is one question that will not be answered.

Charmaine Whitcombe (14)
Coombe Girls' School

Aunties

A unties are great aren't they?
U nderstanding
N ice
T reats me
I nteresting
E xtra energetic

A wesome
L oves playing sport
I ncredibly funny.

Now who has an auntie like that?
Me!

Nicola Giles (11)
Coombe Girls' School

Life's Obstacles

Shouting, screaming what's gone wrong?
Crying, worrying all day long,
I wish this anger would come to an end.

No laughter, no smiles, no smiles at all,
People being picked on if they're too small.
I wish this anger would come to an end,

Poverty, murder, fighting in wars,
Doesn't seem to be for any good cause,
I wish this anger would come to an end.

Different religions, different coloured skin,
Everyone wants to win, win, win!
I wish this anger would come to an end.

Bullying, arguing, friendships coming to an end,
It's just driving me round the bend,
I wish this anger would come to an end.

Hannah Wheatley (13)
Coombe Girls' School

Italian Feast

The pasta boils sitting in the pan,
The bolognese bubbles as fast as it can.
As your mum serves it up on your plate,
You look at it and it reaches your fate.
As it enters your mouth you start to drool,
My mouth starts to turn into a swimming pool.
Hot and juicy is what it is,
This is good enough even for showbiz.
It goes down my throat into the taste boat,
As it enters the stomach it starts to float.
I take another spoonful, again and again,
My taste buds stand up to attention.
I enjoyed the food and I hope you will,
But it still remains my favourite meal.

Charlie Henthorn (12)
Glenthorne High School

Fry Up

I wake up in the morning,
There's a smell in the air.
Breakfast is a-cooking,
I wonder what's there?

Sausages in a frying pan,
Toast upon the grill.
Bacon in the microwave,
Eggy in a pan.

I get myself together,
Adventure down the stairs.
And there upon the table,
My favourite meal stares.

A lovely greasy fry up,
That starts the day off well.
On a cold September morning,
The day I wasn't well.

Emma Wooldridge (12)
Glenthorne High School

Ice Cream

I cannot feel my mouth or tongue
C old as it melts in my mouth
E ating ice cream is like Heaven

C ramming in as much as I can
R eaching in the bottom of the freezer wanting more
E ating quickly with a spoon
A te the rest and still want more
M y mouth tingles with the coldness.

Christopher Emmerson (12)
Glenthorne High School

English Breakfast

E is for egg
N is for nice
G is for grill
L is for lovely English breakfast
I is for irresistible
S is for sausage
H is for hash browns

B is for beans
R is for ready
E is for eaten
A bsolutely delicious
K is for kinda really nice
F is for fried bread
A is for any English breakfast you want
S is for special
T is for tasty tomatoes!

Hayley Cahill (11)
Glenthorne High School

Maltesers

Like hailstones
free-falling from
the sky,

The Maltesers flow
into my mouth,

Mmm . . . malty, crunchy,
crumbly chocolate,

Scrumptious sphere-shaped,
syrupy taste,

Maltesers the chocolate
no one likes to waste.

Laura Knight (12)
Glenthorne High School

Pizza

Pizza is good,
Pizza is nice,
I like mine,
With a hint of spice.

Roll the dough,
Knead it with your knees,
Punch it with your hand,
Then add a bit of cheese.

Add lots of toppings,
Don't forget the ham,
You can even add some bacon,
Just fry it in the pan.

Bake it in the oven,
Until steaming hot,
Take it out,
Are you gonna eat it or not?

Sam Connoley (13)
Glenthorne High School

Food

My favourite food is a curry
It really tastes yummy
I like the rice
It is very nice
And I have it with Coke and ice!

I love the sauce to dip my poppadoms
I sit and eat it in my long johns!
My mum says, 'Don't make a mess!'
I get it all down my vest
But I don't mind, cos I eat the rest!

James Craig (13)
Glenthorne High School

Fruit

Bright and colourful,
Sweet and juicy,
Reds and yellows,
Greens and oranges.

Eat it with a spoon
Or take a lovely bite,
Use your fingers
Or chop it with a knife.

Freshly picked,
Stewed or juiced,
Mixed with ice cream,
Eat them every way.

Limes and lychees,
Apples and apricots,
Peaches and pears,
Mangoes and melons.

Summer fruits,
Citrus fruits,
Tropical fruits,
Fruits of the Earth!

Gabriel Mallows (11)
Glenthorne High School

The Pizza Surprise!

Pizza is a fiery red,
So fiery it burns your tongue.
The pizza is so chewy it makes your mouth water,
Water so much you start dribbling.
The pizza is spicy
So spicy it burns your mouth.
The cheese is stringy
So stringy it swings across your mouth.

Ben Healy (12)
Glenthorne High School

Bon Appétit!

Bon appétit,
Hope you enjoy your food.
Eat it all up, you hungry fellow,
Get it down your gob, dude!
Grab the cod and chips,
The main greasy meal,
Get it down the seaside,
It really is the real deal!
Take that lovely jacket,
The potato kind I mean.
Have it with a piece of cheese
Or maybe Heinz baked beans?
Eat up that roast,
Really not just for Christmas.
Have it on a Sunday,
But not that great with couscous!
So: bon appétit,
Hope you enjoy your food.
Eat it all up, you hungry fellow,
Get it down your gob, dude!

Andrew Bragg (12)
Glenthorne High School

The Latte's

A favourite drink of the adults,
Its chocolate flavours,
Its smooth texture gliding down the throat,
Its velvety feel on the tongue,
Its attractive appearance,
Its frothy cream bouncing on top,
Its subtle brown colour,
Its rich, luxurious smell wafting around the nose
And its neat, sweet mints topped with icing,
Yum, yum!

Megan Pattwell (11)
Glenthorne High School

How To Dive For Pearls And Avoid Eating Your Peas

Remember that peas are pearls
and you are a pearl diver.
Mashed potatoes are coral
and form a tropical lagoon.
The gravy is the ocean
that fills the lagoon.
Drop the pearls into the lagoon.
Dive for pearls.
Surface.
Let the ocean trickle from your chin
and wait to be dismissed
from the table.

Courtney Porter (13)
Glenthorne High School

How Do You Make Pizza Grow?

How do you make a pizza grow?
You pound and you pull and you stretch the dough
and throw in tomatoes and oregano.
Pizza platter for twenty-two
Pour on the oil and soak it through.
Pizza slices for forty-four,
Chop up onions, make some more.
Pizza pie for sixty-six
with mozzarella cheese that melts and sticks.
Pizza, pizza for ninety-nine
with pepperoni sausage ground up fine.
Pizza, pizza, stretches the dough.
Pizza, pizza, makes it grow.

Leslie Apeah (12)
Glenthorne High School

I Hate Vegetables!

I hate vegetables,
I hate fruit,
I hate healthy foods,
So give 'em the boot!

Just give me garbage
And I'll be happy,
I've been eating junk,
Since I was in nappies!

Fatty foods and vile foods,
Just feed me with slop
And if it's not yuck enough,
I'll go to the shop!

So what I'm trying to say is,
Don't feed me that green,
Cos if you do, I'll go to my room
And I'll be really, really mean!

Daniel McNamara (13)
Glenthorne High School

Curly Fries

C urly fries
U sually they disappear before my eyes
R eally crunchy
L ovely and munchy
Y ou can give them to your mates

F ries are yummy
R eally fill my tummy
I love them to bits
E veryone will think they're a hit
S mile and say Curly Fries.

Laura-Jayne Lawton (11)
Glenthorne High School

Milk

I like rice 'cause it tastes nice,
With lots and lots of curry.

I like curry 'cause it smells funny,
With lots and lots of peas.

I like peas 'cause they make me wheeze,
When I choke on them with chips.

I like chips 'cause they tickle my lips,
With lots and lots of beans.

I like beans 'cause they're my favourite greens,
With lots and lots of beef.

I like beef 'cause it sticks in my teeth,
With lots and lots of ice cream.

I like ice cream 'cause it makes me scream,
With lots and lots of tea.

I like tea 'cause it tastes like the sea,
With lots and lots of milk.

Danielle Connor (13)
Glenthorne High School

Custard

C ustard is so delicious for anybody.
U seful with any type of dessert.
S tupendously great for all ages.
T arts with custard are a lovely choice.
A pple crumble goes so well with custard.
R ight with all the puddings.
D airy Milk chocolate with custard on top, you can't beat that!

George Tribe (11)
Glenthorne High School

Ice Poles

It comes in the colours of the rainbow, found at the end.
It's cold upon your taste buds, messages it will send,
Tangy, sweet, sour, smooth
Snowflake flavours it will make you all move,
Easy to eat, all fresh and cool,
Some can even be shaped like a ball!

Mediterranean colours that are just like a sea,
Swirling around and around like it will be,
It cools you down when you are hot,
But on a cold day it will not!
Freezing ice cubes running down your throat,
Swirling around just like a moat.

Jumping around with every crunch to crunch,
Some can make your eyes water with every munch.
A sea-like breeze passing through your mouth,
Sliding down like a stream heading down south,
Easy to buy, easy to make,
It's got to be the icing on the cake,
It's not going to be a scary old troll,
It's going to be the number 1
Ice pole!

Lauren Lewis (13)
Glenthorne High School

I Will Put In My Box . . .
(Based on 'Magic Box' by Kit Wright)

I will put in my box . . .
The stripes of a tiger
The tongue of a mummy
Water from the den of a snake.

I will put in my box . . .
The teeth of a dead man
The toe of the moon
The yellow of the stars.

I will put in my box . . .
The ear of a bird
The moon of Mars
The smell of school dinners.

My box is made with the skin of a snake
The hinges are the nose of Michael Jackson.

I shall play in my box,
And sleep in my box
When the stars are shining.

Dean Stone (13)
Glenthorne High School

I Love To Eat!

I love to eat food,
Don't play with it, that's rude,
Eat lots you should
And eat lots I would.

Don't mind vegetables,
Like to eat fruit
And if anyone touches my food,
I'll give 'em a boot!

Don't eat a lot of junk,
Just stick to breakfast and lunch,
Dinner's a blast, I eat loads and loads,
Eat so much my pants explode!

Love to eat pizza, it's really nice,
So is chicken on top of rice,
Stuffed crust is good, love to eat that,
If it wasn't invented, I'd eat my own hat!

Love to eat when watching TV
And if I laugh then I might choke,
Look mate, you never know,
So I'd push it down with a can of Coke!

Love to eat food,
That's what I just told you,
Anything will satisfy me,
Except broccoli.

Now you know what I like to eat,
Fill me please, fill me up with beef!

Vivek Sharma (13)
Glenthorne High School

A Treat For All!

It looks so neat and tidy,
I don't want to touch it,
Well maybe one bite,

It's melting on my tongue,
My taste buds are dripping,
It's rolling down the back of my throat,
It's so irresistible,

Maybe one piece but no more,
It's like a chocolate river,
From the shallow end to the waterfall,

You're so tempting,
I just can't leave you,
All sitting in a row,
You need to be alone,

I'll help, eat them all up,
I pour them in my mouth,
It's like love at first taste,

You're the only one left, I need you,
I'll save . . . no I won't,
You're lovely,
You're all I need in life,

I need you,
I'll buy more tomorrow
It's so addictive.

Stacey Noble (12)
Glenthorne High School

Sugar Coated, Soft And Chewy!

I love to eat sweets,
They are my favourite treat.
Sugar coated, soft and chewy,
Left in your pocket they'll go all gooey.

Big ones, small ones,
Round ones, square ones,
I could eat tons and tons.

Blue ones, pink ones,
Green ones, white ones,
Eating sweets is really fun.

I could eat them all day through,
Pink ones, white ones, green ones,
Blue.

Leigh Henthorn (13)
Glenthorne High School

Sweets!

Sweets, they make my mouth swing and ping,
Hip-hopping around, doing their thing.
They make me shiver and shake,
Wait, what's that? It's an earthquake.
They're different sizes and shapes,
They've even got their own make.
Loads of colour, blacks and blues,
So many sweets there's nothing to lose.
They got me going so crazy
No, I didn't say lazy.
Some are small and some are big,
Now let's go and get with the jig.

John Casey (12)
Glenthorne High School

Vanilla Ice Cream

The vanilla ice cream was
as refreshing as ice-cold water
being poured over you
on a hot summer day.
Its creamy texture
swirled around my mouth.
The ice cream
melted softly on my taste buds.
Vanilla from the pods of a
tropical plant,
that tastes enjoyable,
like a sunny day.
The vanilla flavour
was a creamy, sweet temptation.
This taste will be in my mouth,
Forever!

Sheriece Bracey (12)
Glenthorne High School

Phish Food Ice Cream!

Phish food ice cream
Oh how I love it
The best food in the world
The caramel is the best bit.

Phish food ice cream
It's not what you think
It's filled with chocolate and fudge
And turns your tongue bright pink.

Phish food ice cream
Oh how I'm glad we met
When it trickles down your throat
It's by far the best you will get.

Katy Godbeer (12)
Glenthorne High School

Lasagne

If you try lasagne,
I swear it won't harm ya!
Lasagne's really nice you know,
I really think you should give it a go!
Lasagne makes me feel so good,
I really want to have it for pud!
Lasagne makes my tummy rumble,
It makes me want to spin, turn and tumble!
When I tumble, spin and turn,
I really hope my lasagne won't burn!

Stacey McDougall (12)
Glenthorne High School

Coffee

C alm and relaxing, guess what? *Coffee*
O riental, decaffe and sweet, guess what? *Coffee*
F ifty pence, five pounds, depends what shop, guess what? *Coffee*
F rothy with sprinkles, guess what? *Coffee*
E ven black or maybe white, still tastes right, guess what? *Coffee*
E ventually you've run out of guess what? *Coffee*

Shauna Curran (14)
Glenthorne High School

My Favourite Food!

Crispy duck, oh what luck,
Crispy pork ball, I could eat them all,
Egg foo yung, tastes lovely on the tongue
Black bean sauce, goes well with your main course
Chicken chow mein, all this you will gain.

Lewis Sawyers (12)
Glenthorne High School

Strawberry

S ucculent silently sitting alone
T asty type of wonderful fruit
R ed raindrops rapidly falling
A lways juicy, the sugar treat
W hether big or small
B right, bold and great
E very time to taste a delight
R eally right to freshen your taste buds
R ed or not ripe
Y ummy, not yuck!

I love strawberries.

Becky Wisdom (13)
Glenthorne High School

Pizza

The hot, crunchy pizza
Was as crumbly as a bread roll
The slightly burnt crust
And the cheesy toppings
Added together make a tasty meal
The stringy cheese and the fire-red tomato
Bursts inside your mouth.

Rachel Stannard (12)
Glenthorne High School

Cakes!

C *heesecake!* Is the best of the bake
A *pple turnover!* Makes your tongue turn over
K *rispie cake!* Is the one you'll take
E *ccles!* Give you freckles
S *trawberry Pavlova!* Cake time is over.

Abbie Studholme (12)
Glenthorne High School

My Food Poem About Pizza

Pizza, pizza, perfect pizza
Thin crust, fat crust
Perfect pizza
Pepperoni, diced or sliced
Different toppings
What you like.

Pizza, pizza, perfect pizza
Margherita slice
Extra cheese is what you need
For the perfect slice.

Pizza, pizza, perfect pizza
Wedges on the side
Spicy, normal, whatever you like
With your perfect pizza.

George Hellewell (11)
Glenthorne High School

Ribs, Rice And Sauce

I love ribs, rice and sauce,
when I put it in my hands, it's all greasy,
I could eat them all day,
full of sauce they're all tasty
and I finally put my teeth through the meat
and rip like a lion through an antelope,
they're delicious, I recommend them to anybody
and you can share my love,
for those meat on bones snacks,
from all good supermarkets,
you can buy nice little 20 packs.

Lucas Willmott (12)
Glenthorne High School

Chomping Chocolate

Chocolate, chocolate in my mouth,
Makes me happy, makes me shout.

I'll have one or maybe two,
All for me and none for you.

Minute sizes are not all right,
Colossal sizes for me to bite.

I could munch a bar of choc,
From morning to 12 o'clock.

Chomping chocolate is not a joke,
I'd have it more than sweets or Coke.

But remember, don't eat it too quick,
Eat too much and you'll be sick.

Caroline Flinders (13)
Glenthorne High School

A Poem About Poems!

When my pen meets the paper,
My head lights up like a burning taper.

Then I write down my dreams and wishes,
Then I eat my favourite dishes.

Then I get someone with dictation,
Adding my own punctuation.

Starting with a capital letter at the beginning of every line,
Now it's time to finish the rhyme.

Checking my spelling as I write,
Making sure it sounds right.

Ending lines with full stops,
Just until my head drops!

Thomas Yelf (13)
Glenthorne High School

Chinese

This is my poem about Chinese
the succulent, spicy spare ribs sizzle my insides
the dazzling, diced duck runs down my throat like liquid gold
but of course the best dish of all
the tasty sweet chicken balls
to top it off a nice ice cream
when it's gone I'm so sad I scream.
Just typical of me
so easy to see
I forgot some of the main parts
the ones that stay true to my heart
the egg fried rice, the chicken chow mein
but I don't like the veggies they're way too lame
I'm sad when I'm not there
I'm glad in mine I've never found a hair
now it's time to end this exquisite poem about food
now please watch your remarks, do not be rude.

Jamie Hall (12)
Glenthorne High School

Meal Time

The thin egg slices slide onto your tongue
Whilst the cheese melts onto your teeth.

The burnt edges crisp when your teeth
Break into the hot, steaming mince.

Your mind just focuses on your dinner
More than anything else.

You take your time eating and by the time
You get to the last strip
The whole hotness has faded away into the distance.

Megan Thoroughgood (12)
Glenthorne High School

Chocolate

My favourite food is chocolate,
I like it most when it's in my tummy,
white or milk it's all yummy.
I like it most when there's lots and lots,
I really don't mind if there's stripes or dots.
My favourite food is chocolate,
big bars or little bars,
wrappers or jars,
I really don't mind,
As long as it's not hard to find.
My favourite food is chocolate,
whatever size, whatever shape,
whatever make, whatever name,
I really don't mind.
My favourite food is chocolate.

Hannah Jeffries (13)
Glenthorne High School

That's Why I Like Cake

Strawberry cake
Raspberry cake
Orange cake
Toffee cake
That's why I like cake,
Double cake,
Chocolate cake
Fruit cake
That's why I like cake,
Belgian cake,
Sweet cake
Truffle cake
Shortbread cake
That's why I like cake.

Daniel Gregory (13)
Glenthorne High School

Song Of Myself/Look After Life

Death will come when death will please and why should I complain
For I have felt the winter cold and smelt the summer rain.
However, life has more to give, there's more to learn each day,
So I will not yet sacrifice tomorrow or today.

I still have paths to follow and paths that I regret,
I have hopes and dreams and fears and problems to forget.
I'm part of the youth of 2004, I have miles and miles to go,
When I am old and life is ending, I'll know all I need to know.

Two hands, two feet, a body blessed, for this gift I'm full of thanks,
Some people in the world I live, their lives are just plain blank.
A shelter at night, the right to be free,
No hunger or pain and no slavery.

I feel for the people who live in despair,
Who travel through life with no love or no care.
A world that has wrongs, a world that has bad,
But most of my life is happy, not sad.

I value my wisdom, my family and friends,
The people who love me, on them I depend.
The opportunities and chances that are available to me,
Will make my future a happy one and successful I will be.

When the end is within my reach,
My message to all that I will teach.
Within each day that you are blessed,
Take your time to do your best.
Follow your dreams and aim at the sky,
'Cause then you'll rest in peace when you die.

Lauren Payne (13)
Glenthorne High School

My Favourite Song

I'm happy about myself;
For what I do - you may do it the same
And I'm just like everyone else . . . but just a bit different.

I like my character and myself alongside my hobbies
And always do it my way with a touch of delicacy.

My room is always full of fresh air with the windows wide open,
I'm relaxed to know where I am and why I'm there,
Sometimes I get carried away by my work - sometimes . . .

I'm like every teenager in the world, but with my own personality,
I like the sweet aroma of nature,
With a touch of rain from the blue coloured sky,
Alongside a stunning rainbow right in front of the picture.
Maybe I like games,
Swimming in a blue lagoon with a sandy beach,
A certain kind of music when I'm working,
Hanging out with my friends in the middle of the night with a smell of
perfume and utter silence.
A wide-screen TV with cartoons and documentaries.

All this is a small part of my daily routine - but . . .

Have you given a thought about your future and your life?
Have you trained that hard to perfection and to achieve something?
Have you got what it takes to fulfil your own potential?

Everything goes onward and never backwards in life . . .
But you'll be able to make it that one bit better,
For if you do, you'll be different, and . . . luckier!

Dakordass Tengur (13)
Glenthorne High School

Apple

Shiny and round,
Be sure to not drop it on the ground
So juicy and sweet,
Good enough for you to eat.

Leave it too long and it will go soft,
You can eat them anywhere even in your loft,
Don't be afraid to try,
After one they will all go by.

They're red or green,
Very few people eat red,
Well, that's what other people have said.

They're a type of fruit,
Worms like apples too,
Let's just hope it's not the same one as you!

Hannah Whitehead (11)
Glenthorne High School

Chips, Chips

Chips, chips
They're my power
I'll eat them and eat them past the hour
Some short, some small
Some burnt, that's disgraceful
Salt and vinegar
They're they key
To the fantastic
Taste of the sea
The chips go on my tongue
The tastebuds have fun
Then the enzymes come
By the ton
Chips, chips
They're my power
I'll eat them and eat them past the hour.

Russell Wells (13)
Glenthorne High School

Smarties

Smarties, they're great,
Smarties, they're fun,
Lots of Smarties for everyone.

Orange, green, red and yellow,
Melted Smarties are nice and mellow,
Purple, pink, brown and blue,
They're my favourite, how about you?

When I go to the corner shop,
I look at the sweets and then I stop,
No competition, it's easy for me,
Smarties all the way, continually.

Morning, noon, lunch and night,
For me the Smarties are beautifully right,
I really can't help it, I love them so much,
The swirled chocolate smell and the soft golden touch.

So Smarties are great,
Smarties are fun,
Loads of Smarties for everyone.

Megan King (12)
Glenthorne High School

Sweets

I enjoy the fizziness biting my taste buds
I enjoy eating them all year long
It's my favourite shop and I eat them a lot
Did you guess?
Yes
It's the sweet shop.

I like the fizziness clashing and smashing around my mouth
I like them so sour they make my eyes water.

Chris Sayers (12)
Glenthorne High School

The Worry Week

Beware Monday,
It creaks and shakes,
It drives you through roundabouts,
It stands up tall and smart
And it might play your part.

Beware Tuesday,
It may give you a fright
And always think it's right,
It is very small,
But it isn't no fool.

Beware Wednesday,
It coughs and sniffles,
It won't play games, but might tickle,
It can be harsh,
It could trap you in its soggy marsh.

Beware Thursday,
A dark and dingy day,
To bark up its tree is the wrong way,
It will threaten you,
So to mess it isn't good to do.

Beware Friday,
It is now coming for you with many weapons,
It will get you as fast as a leopard,
They way it moves,
The way it soothes.

Beware Saturday,
The way it screams,
He stands as hollow as beams,
Get out as soon as you can,
Because when he does, you ran.

Beware Sunday,
The end of terror,
If you survive which half, the time is never,
It will finish you off,
Because if you will, he will hear you cough.

Jamie Clayton (13)
Glenthorne High School

My Life

My life;
A series of ups and downs,
A series of changes.

I have done lots of things in my life,
I have made many mistakes.
I have had many friends,
I have lost relatives.
My life;
A series of ups and downs,
A series of changes.

My school is a place of achievement for all who wish to achieve;
Long and hard, I have worked to achieve.
Long and hard, I have worked to the best of my ability.
Long and hard, I have worked to make my parents proud. And I have.
My life;
A series of ups and downs,
A series of changes.

One human among billions of others.
What makes me special?
Nothing. A blade of grass, a flower, an ice cube, a single leaf.
What makes them special?
Nothing. But they can be special and so can I.

That's my life;
A series of ups and downs,
A series of changes,
A life of great happiness.

Anthony Fagan (13)
Glenthorne High School

Orange Evening!

I pick up into my own selfless bare hands,
Then my whole mouth expands.

The smell just makes me want to cry,
For another treacle tart, I would die!

I dearly love this orange delight,
When I look at it, it's such a sight,
It's so lovely to crunch and munch,
I could eat all these till lunch!
Oh! Do I love treacle tart,
Baking these tarts must be such art,
Swallow my entire love,
This tart is more prettier than a dove,
Would you look at the time!
This is the last rhyme.

Sean Murphy (12)
Glenthorne High School

Carrots

Carrots are orange
Carrots are long
Carrots are smelly
And make you grow big and strong.
Carrots are colourful
They look really nice
Carrots are lovely
And go well with rice.
Dig them up
Put them on a plate
Have them for dinner
Or when you come home late.

Kiran Williams (13)
Glenthorne High School

Chocolate

The scrumptious, sweet sensation melting in my mouth!
The tasty, tantalising taste twirling round and round!
In my mouth the chocolate swirls like water in a river!
No other sweet or savoury snack would send my back to shiver!

The scrumptious, sweet sensation melting in my mouth!
The priceless piece of pleasure making taste buds feel left out!
The colour of my chocolate would never put me off
Even the cheapo chocolate shouldn't be shared with a sloth!

The scrumptious, sweet sensation melting in my mouth!
Cadburys, Galaxy and even Mars make others feel left out!
I really need my chocolate so give it to me *now!*
You better give me chocolate or I really will just *shout!*

Michelle Easton (12)
Glenthorne High School

Cherry

Cherries, cherries, very red cherries,
You can't compare a cherry to any other berry.

They might be dipped in syrup and bitten off their stalk,
They could be munched as you play and talk.

They come in purple or a bright red,
I eat them so much, they're going to my head.

When I chew them I feel utter bliss,
Their colour reminds me of a red rose kiss.

These small, little fruits I love to devour,
I could eat a pile, higher than the Eiffel Tower.

Now I've come to the end of this song,
You now must know that cherries aren't wrong.

Scott Nicholls (12)
Glenthorne High School

Chinese!

My favourite food is Chinese,
Special fried rice is tasty and also very nice,
It makes my mouth water with the taste of spice,
Spare ribs in barbecue sauce are great,
With the sticky mess they make!
But overall, crispy duck with pancakes
Is my best choice of all!

Emily Bullimore (12)
Glenthorne High School

Chocolate

C oloured chocolate
H ard when you bite it
O range chocolate
C oconut chocolate
O h so delicious
L arge bars
A lways yummy
T ongue-tastic
E ating it all day!

Jo Hannah (13)
Glenthorne High School

Curry

I love curry
I love the way the spices tickle your tongue
I love the way the chillies leave your face numb
I love the way the poppadoms crackle in your mouth
I love the way the sauce soothes your tummy.
I love curry!

Harry Knock (12)
Glenthorne High School

Apples

Umm! Let me tell you about apples,
Apples are delicious,
Apples have that mouth-watering taste,
As you crunch into the middle,
You can feel and taste the fruit of an exotic island,
Apples are refreshing when it's a hot day and you're feeling down,
Apples taste sweet and are a sugary type of fruit.

Apples are fun for everyone!
Holly Ellemarie Richards (11)
Glenthorne High School

The Olive

Pitted black olives are to die for,
I have them on pizza and I want more, more, more.
Green or black, round and small,
They're good with a salad or any meal at all.
They come in tins, sometimes in jars,
You buy them in Tesco, but not in bars.
So if you're hungry and feeling blue,
Remember the olive, it's good for you!

Daniel Kyprianou (12)
Glenthorne High School

Madras

M edium hot
A mber or orangey colour
D elicious and
R ich flavours
A tmosphere of the Indian restaurant
S mells that make you feel hungry.

Sara Druce (12)
Glenthorne High School

Meat Feast

The pizza was as rough as a rocky road
It felt like I was in a trance or even a mode.

The round frame was the shape of the moon
No one can eat it with a spoon.

It is maisonette, mouth-watering, moving, pouncing on my buds
A tornado meat feast coiling in my mouth, it's scrumptious.

The red blood colour, it almost scared me
Me and pizza are meant to be.

Alex Dawson (12)
Glenthorne High School

Chocolate

C runchy and creamy,
H ot and heavy,
O ozing with strawberries,
C hunky with caramel,
O h so lovely,
L ooking nice with Smarties,
A te it with a friend I think it's,
T oo good to share, so it was . . .
E aten within seconds, not a crumb left.

Vida Kohan Ghadr (13)
Glenthorne High School

Apple

A nice crunch with juice inside
P eople can eat them anywhere.
    You don't need a plate, a knife or a fork
P eople can eat them whenever they like
L ovely and juicy when you eat them
E njoy a nice piece of crunchy fruit.

Dean Saunders (13)
Glenthorne High School

Chocolate

C hewy and yummy
H eavenly taste
O pen the packet
C an't share the rest
O nly thing to eat
L ovely melted
A nd always cheap
T aste's the best
E at none of the rest.

Stephanie Dutton (14)
Glenthorne High School

Ice Cream

I cy-cold taste in your mouth,
C hocolate flavour is the best,
E veryone likes it

C reamy, really smooth,
R eally tasty, no one can resist it,
E at in summer or winter if you like,
A lways gives you brain freeze,
M elts as soon as it's in your mouth.

Zoe Thaxter (14)
Glenthorne High School

Plums

P urple plums
L ovely and juicy
U nder the trees we eat our plums
M y mates like them too
S ome are nicer than others.

Dean Stone (13)
Glenthorne High School

Spaghetti Hoops

Spaghetti hoops are tomatoey and tangy
Spaghetti hoops are slimy and saucy
Spaghetti hoops are red and round
Spaghetti hoops are soft and sizzling
Spaghetti hoops are juicy and tasty
Spaghetti hoops are yellow and yummy
Spaghetti hoops are groovy and gappy
Spaghetti hoops are shaped like a Polo.

Ashleigh Gaynor (13)
Glenthorne High School

Spaghetti And Pasta

S paghetti is lovely,
P asta is great,
A lways fills my tummy,
G ood food on my plate,
H eats up in no time,
E at it with a sauce,
T hink - what is your favourite?
T omato of course,
I love it!

Emma Martin (12)
Glenthorne High School

Apple

A very hard piece of food
P eople eat it on a diet
P eel it or eat it with the skin on
L ike a little baseball
E dible and tastes real good.

Scott Mitchell (13)
Glenthorne High School

Chocolate

C reamy, crunchy and delicious
H ow much I want it now
O h I could smell its chocolaty smell
C hocolate! Chocolate!
O h, yum yum!
L ight brown and milky
A big, creamy chocolate, mmmmm!
T reasure is nothing compared to chocolate
E at it while it lasts!

Gisele Nishimwe (13)
Glenthorne High School

Sweets Are . . .

Scrumptious, fruity, tangy, mine,
Sweets are sugary, sour, so fine.

They're pinky, greeny, bluey, weenie,
Smarties are so tasteful and teeny.

The sour blast zaps my tongue,
My taste buds boogie and have some fun.

I love sweets lots, I love them loads,
I hate my parents when they say, 'No!'

Tommy Prescott (13)
Glenthorne High School

Pasta

Pasta is soft and slimy
Pasta is green and gooey
Pasta is twirly and tangy
Pasta is yellow and yummy
Pasta is red and round
Pasta looks like a slug.

Louise Larter (13)
Glenthorne High School

Chuppa Chups Lollipop

Lollipop, lollipop is my favourite sweet,
Lollipop, lollipop is what I like to eat,
Lollipop, lollipop is the best thing ever,
Lollipop, lollipop I'll never share them, never!

Lollipop, lollipop is lovely and juicy,
Lollipop, lollipop is colourful and fruity,
Lollipop, lollipop I take them wherever I go,
Lollipop, lollipop I love them, don't you know!

Seher Bellikli (11)
Glenthorne High School

Jam Tarts

J is for just delicious
A is for appetising
M is for more, more, more

T is for tasty
A is for any time
R is for raspberry
T is for two, one is not enough
S is for satisfied.

Tiffany Mok (11)
Glenthorne High School

Jelly

J elly tastes really nice,
E verybody have a slice,
L ovely jubbly, it's really lovely,
L ots of jelly goes in my tummy,
Y ou all know jelly goes wibbly wobbly on the plate!

Chloe Miller (12)
Glenthorne High School

Food

It tastes so good, so good to eat,
Chocolate, crisps are such a treat,
Bread, salads, pasta too,
Chocolate, toffee cake covered in goo,
Salads and fruit, so good for you,
Jacket potatoes, boiled and new,
All these foods we eat each day,
Before we come to school and during play,
A little of each is good for you,
But not the chocolate, all the things I love too!

Danielle Jade Davies (13)
Glenthorne High School

Crisps

C runchy crisps in my mouth,
R eally tasty, loads of flavours,
I ndigo, red, blue and green,
 these are the colours of the packets, they gleam,
S alty and cheesy to lamb and mint sauce,
P acketed and sent all over the world,
S traight into my mouth - mmmm great!

Charlie Gummer (13)
Glenthorne High School

Chocolate

Dairy Milk, Milky Way, Galaxy makes my day,
Creamy, milky, swirly chocolate,
Caramel, Maltesers, Kit-Kat, Crunchie,
How it's so munchie!
Oh how I love chocolate,
Oh how I love to eat chocolate!

Claire Hossack (11)
Glenthorne High School

Chocolate

C runches in our mouths,
H ard as stone,
O h the sweet smell as it melts,
C hocolate cake
O h the soft and powdery texture
L ovely and smooth
A mazing taste
T housands of people
E ggs at Easter.

Caroline Stakalls (13)
Glenthorne High School

Fudge!

Fudge, fudge, glorious fudge.
It smells delicious
And tastes so sweet.
I want to eat it all day long.
Fudge!

Fudge, fudge, glorious fudge.
I have always loved it
And I love the vanilla one the most
I couldn't live without it.
Fudge!

Emma Marlow (12)
Glenthorne High School

Cheese

C heese comes in all different makes,
H ealthy, delicious, goes nicely with grapes,
E ver so tempting in all sorts of shapes,
E dible, tasty and easily grates,
S o much healthier than eating cakes,
E ven in the oven, it's delicious when baked!

Natasha Hall (14)
Glenthorne High School

Sausages

Fried eggs, sizzling,
Boiled eggs, bubbling,
Poached eggs rising,
Scrambled eggs, mushing,
Sausages, screaming,
While they're flying.

Bacon, burning,
While it's turning,
This is my full English breakfast.

Haydon Godbeer (12)
Glenthorne High School

Pancakes

P is for pancakes
A is for amazement
N is for never being nasty
C is for crazy, fun, flipping
A is for a great laugh
K is for keep them in the pan
E is for exciting
S is for sugar.

Natalie Morisse (12)
Glenthorne High School

What Is It?

They're as red as blood
Sweet as sugar candy
They're as small as a mouse
The juice river swirled in my mouth
Its smooth texture tickled my tongue
Can you guess what it is?
A cherry!

Holly Simmons (12)
Glenthorne High School

Why You?

Why I can't say
I love you.
Why I dream about you
And I can't sleep.
Why I am cross
When you smile to another.
Why I think about you all the time,
About your eyes and how you smile.
Why when I look to the stars
I am thinking about you.

Your smile
Like a baby.
Sweet kiss
Like a chocolate
Feeling warm
In my heart,
Like a volcano coming here.
Don't make me jealous
Or hurt me.
Love doesn't hurt.
It makes me and you
Love forever.

Yes, I love you
But why I can't say it.
Why I can't say
I love you.
Why?

Wafa Hussein (13)
Haling Manor High School

Stuck In A Maze

Nicotine, alcohol, drugs,
Addiction is like a maze . . . maze . . . maze
You don't know what corner to turn, or path to take
Nobody realises how close the exit is
Some never find the exit that's because
They choose not to
They are cornered into a dead end -
And trapped forever
How do you get trapped into the maze in the first place?
Boredom, experimenting, socialising, mates
Buying in . . . and that's 'well dear'

What makes you stay in the maze?
'It makes the day go quicker'
'It's easy, the temptation's there'
'The buzz is good.'
'Pity there's no way else of getting that buzz'

You can get out of the maze,
Finding the exit is hard, that's true!
There's no doubt about it!
To find the exit you need help but will you take it?
Some people get out by luck, others by cheating
The best way out is willpower but have you got it?

You have to choose to quit the buzz,
You have to choose health and life
You have to choose the straight path to the future.

George McConnachie (15)
Pyrford Centre

The Amazing Hero
(Inspired by Michael Rosen)

Today in class
I *read* the poem out in class from start to finish,
I *listened* to the teacher,
And did all the *work*
I didn't walk out, not even when
The other students walked out,
I was *amazing* today
Amazing,
Amazing, amazing,
Amazing.

Shane Cummins (15)
Pyrford Centre

Lost

As I see her lying there
I feel a surge of love,
She makes me feel safe.

But she's slipping away,
Slowly, slowly.

The nurses come in to take her away,
My heart, it breaks,
I see my tears on her sweet face.

My father comes in to take me away,
I don't want to leave, to leave her alone,
She won't like it, I know she won't,
I feel I should stay with her.

I can feel myself struggling half-heartedly because
I know I must let her be,
To leave her in peace.

Goodbye Mother.

Hannah Tiernan (12)
Sutton High School

The Hunger Of Africa

Creeping slyly through the long parched grass,
Waiting, longing, for prey that does not come,
The hot sun curses the thirsty creatures
Of this desperate, dying land.

Fast, weak breath comes from the mouth
Of the patient, lonely being,
The jagged edges of the shade cast from the acacia tree
Encircles the waiting animal.

Its ribs jut out of the stunning blanket of fur,
Its tongue from between the sharp pearls of teeth,
Graceful, angry, striking, distressed,
The waiting goes on.

The perfect African sky - spotless, invariable
Like an artists' untouched masterpiece
Rests above the silent expanse
Of this desperate, dying land.

Katrina Watson (14)
Sutton High School

The Importance Of Happiness

A crisp sweet smile,
Will help all the while.
Just let it linger,
Keep it there as sweet as ginger.
Some see your smile,
And help all the while.
By dressing in their best grin,
A smile so lovely, their life to begin.

Your smile makes a lot of people happy,
That is why we are here,
To spread happiness,
So take heed of my advice,
And trust my words when I say,
'Enjoy life and spread happiness!'

Alexandra Sadler (12)
Sutton High School

Summer

Green leaves and summer flowers make her dress of
Pink, green, yellow and white,
Whilst her blonde flowing hair reflects the sun's light,
On her back she wears a pair of beautiful wings,
And round her ankles she has bells which ring.

She is full of life
And every man's ideal wife,
She is happy and light-hearted,
And from us she will never be parted.

She scatters the world with love,
As strong and meaningful as the peace of a dove,
She sends out warmth and heat,
Which grows the wheat for people to eat.

She always smells fruity,
And if she were visible you would be astounded by her beauty,
She would never hesitate to share,
And for the sick she will always care.

When autumn comes,
And the children have eaten all the plums,
She fades away,
And hides until next May.

Then she will have another birth,
And come back to us on Earth,
And whilst she is gone, I'm sure you'll find,
She is a wonderful gift to mankind.

Lucy Rhiannon Penwarden (15)
Sutton High School

Eat Your Greens

There was a girl whose name was Jean,
She ate sweets but not her greens,
Every supper her mother would scream,
'Silly girl - just eat your greens.'

Every night Jean would ignore her mother,
And so began the war,
To prove a point Jean stopped eating veg and fruit - the lot!
As Jean matured into a teen,
She still did not eat her greens.
Her mother was still always keen to tell her,
'If you don't eat your greens, you'll turn into a green monster,'
Then one day on her 18th birthday, she looked in the mirror
And what did she say?
'Oh Heavens just look at me!
I've turned into a great green pea.'
Her mother shouted, yelled and screamed,
'I told you what would happen if you neglected your greens,;
When she was forced to enter the street,
What creature did she unfortunately meet?

A big healthy ogre who had an appetite,
He thought, *why don't I take a bite,*
This is the story of little Jean
Says the monster! 'I eat my greens!'

Elizabeth Yentumi (12)
Sutton High School

The Guardians Of Life

The heat boils upon my skin,
I feel myself growing dizzy,
Water, how I yearn for it,
How such a simple thing that meant nothing
Now means everything.

Water all around me,
In a constant shower from above,
It penetrates through your skin into your thoughts,
Spreading icy cold and sadness,
Making you yearn for heat.

The heat lies still around me,
Making me hazy and hot,
There's no water, no movement, no noise,
There is no escaping it,
You have to face it.

Snow is everywhere you look,
Beautiful and marvellous for a little while,
Then it turns into a destructive beast,
Ruining everything in its path,
Leaving no heat or happiness.

Both heat and water are the same,
Some love it, others hate it,
They live in almost opposite worlds,
But both play a key part in the circle of life,
Both give and take life.

Sophie Kavanagh (12)
Sutton High School

Home

Time for home now, leave the school,
Dawdling out slowly to get in the car,
Slump on the back seat, stretching out,
Dump your bag on the front door mat.

Time for fun now, sit down slowly,
See what's on the TV,
Relaxing feels so good yet so bad,
There's a sea of homework in your bag,
Waiting for you to dive in and drown.

Time for homework now, dig in the bag,
Shuffle the books careful like cards,
Decide which torture to start first,
Maths, French, a little history,
Leave it until after dinner.

Dinnertime now, food hot on the table,
Freshly cooked and golden brown,
Plates piled high, cutlery at the sides,
Sit down quickly and add a dash of salt,
Take a big bite of steaming goodness.

Time for bed now, climb the stairs,
Get ready slowly, there's no rush now,
Brush your teeth and have a bath,
Get into bed, say goodnight,
Close your eyes and get ready to start,

Again.

Lucy Yaqub (12)
Sutton High School

Bullet Of Death

Howling winds
Flowing from ear to ear
Ranting and raving
Rupturing my insides,

The bullet encased in my flesh
Slitting my sinews
My thread of life
Dangling above me,

Slashed in half
There I lay
Drowning in my own fate
Blood seeping through my world,

The pain ceases
My life torn
I lay my head forever
As God rest my soul.

Indresh Umaichelvam (14)
Sutton High School

DIY

My dad likes DIY,
He hits nails, but always lets out a sigh,
Because he smacks his hand.

He can work for days,
But it never ever pays,
Because even my mum can do it quicker.

He really loves DIY,
And is always willing to try,
Because my dad and DIY
Go together like cream and apple pie.

Meghan Tomacki (15)
Sutton High School

The Girl

The girl with blonde hair
Swaying from side to side,
But her face so hideous,
No one can stare,
She smiles at me,
I look away,
She comes closer and closer until . . .
I feel her long golden hair sealed against my fair face.
There so soft, so tender, so mellow,
That I fall into it and drop onto her,
I soon realise I'm on her,
My heart begins to race!
I scream (in my head)
Not knowing what to do I stand up and run away,
She looks so confused,
But smiles and walks on by.

Sheryl Ann Odame (11)
Sutton High School

Imagine

Imagine a defenceless, intimidated fox cub,
It had done nothing sinful or vicious,
The hunters had just been teetering on the edge of luck,
Before locating this innocent cub.
And now, he was dashing down the hillside,
Tail between his legs,
More horrified than he knew how to be,
The countryside flashing past became a blur,
The second last thing he heard was a voice,
A voice to chill the bone marrow,
A voice of hissing venom, 'After him!'
The last thing he heard was the crazy yapping,
Barely focused, he saw the hounds,
Then he knew no more.

Amy Rosier (11)
Sutton High School

What's The Point In My Life? From 'I Am David'

Listening to the howling wind,
I lay silently crying,
Had I come to the end?
I couldn't ask God to save me.

Feeling as good as dead,
A blanket of snow slowly covered me,
There was no more beauty,
I had no hope left,
No dreams left!

Maria filled my mind as I shivered,
I felt as good as blind,
As I squinted in the darkness,
My fears flooded back to me,
As I lay cold and still in the gloom.

Charlotte Trefusis (11)
Sutton High School

How To Make A Frosty Fizz Cocktail

First add a cup brimming with excitement,
That fizzes intensely with a sense of ambition.
Next add the cool and sweet juices of co-operation,
That blend together to create an efficient team.
Then pour some willpower into the concoction,
To make the outcome become sweeter and worthwhile,
Follow this with a pinch of experimentation,
That is sure to give your drink an individual taste.
Don't forget to also add a substantial amount of hard work,
Which is essential for any task you wish to pioneer.
Add a slice of hope to sit delicately on the rim,
And then frost the glass with a coating of glamour,
Then sprinkle in a tablespoon of anticipation,
Coupled with the sweet taste of success and triumph.
And finally lace the drink with the sharp taste of realisation,
That a messy kitchen is waiting to be cleaned!

Grishma Shanbhag (13)
Sutton High School

Stiperstones

Don't go walking in the mountains
Don't go near the Stiperstones
See the hedge of blackened hawthorn
Writhe and twist like ancient bones.

Watch the mist curl ever closer
See the stones that sit and wait
Too late for moonlight
Turn and meet your fate.

Hear your footsteps echo, echo
With darkness crawling nearer
Whispering your fate
Their voices growing clearer.

Huge rocks rise on the skyline
Loud the wind roars in your ears
Stiperstones are calling, calling
Down the echoes of the years.

Lie down and forget your sorrow
Let your troubles flow away
None will know you've gone tomorrow
Vanished with the break of day.

Don't go walking in the mountains
Don't go near the Stiperstones
See the hedge of ancient hawthorn
Writhe and twist like blackened bones.

Emma Dee (11)
Sutton High School

The Sea

How I wish I was the sea,
With not a care in the world,
The sun shining on me by day,
And the moon by night.

When I'm angry,
I could build up a wave,
Smash it down,
Onto the houses below.

But if I'm happy,
I could let the people swim,
In and out of my blueness,
Laugh and play in the sand at my feet,
And relax with my waves washing over them.

If I was the sea, it would be great,
I'd have an eternal life,
Inviting fish to swim
In the seaweed and coral beneath me.

At last I would be able
To see the mermaids
I would be their only protection,
And also their home.

I wish I was the sea!

Cara Marguerite Hyde (11)
Sutton High School

Getting Ready

The girls are all looking fantastic
Wearing dresses all made from elastic
And bracelets of metal and plastic
There's a house party this Friday night.

There are boys that they're thinking of pleasing
All night drinking and winking and teasing
And they're sure there'll be hugging and squeezing
At the house party this Friday night.

Now the lip gloss is steadily flowing
And the hairdryer's constantly blowing
Added tissue stops bosoms plateauing
At the house party this Friday night.

It is Cara's mascara they're using
All applied - there is confidence oozing
Mum and Dad hope there will be no boozing
At the house party this Friday night.

It is now time to go - spirit's rising
They look gorgeous which isn't surprising!
And they hope of sensationalising
At the house party this Friday night.

They arrive - the boys think they're fantastic
In their dresses all made of elastic
It's such fun - they are enthusiastic
At the house party this Friday night.

Annabel Reed (15)
Sutton High School

Space

The swirling vortex in front of me
Sucking me up and spitting me out
Into another dimension I fall
Waiting for the bump when I land.

Gasping for breath in this empty world
There's no one anywhere to be seen
I'm stranded, I'm all alone
Nothing here is green.

Oh how I miss the bright warm sun
Shining in the sky
The birds that twitter every morning
The smell of the rhubarb pie.

Here everything is cold and dark
So quiet and strange and lonely
I'm worried and scared, I don't fit in with this landscape
I've made a home but it doesn't feel homely.

I'm stranded here
I'll never get back
It's the darkness I fear
And it's the food I lack.

Nicola Hensley (11)
Sutton High School

Chocolate Cake

A brown looking sweet pyramid,
Packed in a tin with a shiny lid,
The chocolate swirls go round and round,
While 'give me cake' the children hound!
Up and down roll their eyes,
Nobody's touching it, there it lies,
As the lady shares it out,
Everyone leans forward, jumping up and about.

Shruti Jhalla (12)
Sutton High School

An Evocation

The old men cry and turn to stone,
Marbled on a funeral throne;
Their arms blood red with tears of pain,
Show the dagger's scarlet stain;
The cities' streets are live with flame,
Subway walls show who's to blame,
And terror lifts its deadly mask,
Acting out its woeful task.

The graves lie deep with tears of shame,
As life concedes its solemn claim,
And heavy lies the captive heart,
Knowing anguish due to start;
And in the shadow mists of time,
Old men live again the crime,
And know there's nothing they can do,
To make the tale start anew.

Maria Pierides (16)
Sutton High School

An Autumn Scene

The spider spins a web which tells a tale,
To match the grass, glistening with dew.
The holly and mistletoe start to bud,
The story of autumn has begun.

Trees become bare,
Their dignity in piles,
Jumped into by children,
With a crackle, and a snap.

Chestnuts collected to roast,
On a fire made from cut down trees,
As family gather round,
With the scent of bonfire in their hair.

Charlotte Irvine (12)
Sutton High School

Messages Through The Skies

The cold season strikes back,
Again!
The longest of them all . . .
Cold, dreary winter

Leaves tossed along the streets,
Lifeless trees,
Withering in the cold,
Dried flowers, shattered to the ground,

Dark clouds filling the skies,
Animals trying to hibernate,
But the harsh winds awaken them,
And cold gusts of wind attack,

Life comes to a halt in winter,
But the flickering flame keeps burning,
For that one sparkling glow that changed the Earth,
The birth of Christ, our Lord.

Niresha Umaichelvam (11)
Sutton High School

Autumn

Crisp brown leaves lay on the ground,
Layer upon layer,
The weather gets colder,
The days get shorter.

One lonely leaf won't let go,
Of the warm summer it had before,
The winter wind blows hard,
It joins its family in the watery mush.

The life is squished out of the little fellow
As each foot stamps and stamps,
You hear the faint scream
As the body liquids rush out.

Lauren Williamson (12)
Sutton High School

The Woods

The hill stands solemn and isolated,
Silence is broken by the howling of the wolf in the woods.
The trees are shivering as the moon gleams with joy,
The trees whisper to the screeching wind.

The fireflies drift aimlessly through the leaves,
The branches are woven together in a muddle,
The grass is sticking up like towers.

A spider scuttles out and tries to find its way in the gloomy darkness,
A bird swoops and grabs the spider,
He flies up and gets caught in the entwined system of the leaves.

Bats pierce the air like a knife, stooping and swerving like acrobats.

A dark figure darkens the deepest part of the woods,
The shrivelled flowers crunch defensively as they are stepped on,
A rustle of leaves wakes the bear,
Slowly rising and falling with the poisonous dart.

A loud thump shakes the trees' bones,
The bush crackled, disgruntled as if in pain,
The heavy figure rushes its new buds,
The wind swishes to the animals as they circle, waiting.

Sophie Dix (12)
Sutton High School

Holidays

Finally the day has come,
The summer break has just begun.
Many people will take the plane,
To their chosen foreign terrain.
I will travel in my trusty car,
To a place not so very far.
It may only be our English Devon
But to me it is my ideal Heaven.

Lara Battinson (12)
Sutton High School

I Don't Understand

It's mental not physical pain
You've done it before and you're doing it again
Try and explain to me what you have to gain
'Cause I don't understand what I've done.

The bad things you say hurt
You treat me like dirt
And I am not likely to forget
But I don't understand what I've done.

You gang up on me with your crew
And I don't know what to do
I know I can't win when you have them
I just don't understand what I've done.

I hate the sound of you coming
'Cause I know what you are going to do
I know there is no point in running
You would just run after me too
Though I don't understand what I've done.

It's coming to an end now you begin to walk away
It's only for now, as you have run out of things to say
You'll be back tomorrow as it's just another day
I don't understand what I've done.

Harriet Hewett (14)
Sutton High School

Chocolate

Anticipation,
Shiny skin, graphic-etched,
Glinting in the afternoon sunlight,
Beckoning.

Trembling fingers reach out,
Skin split down one side,
With a satisfying ripping sound.
The soul beneath revealed -
Cut to perfection
And gently grooved
At precise intervals.

That long-remembered aroma;
Bitter; sweet,
Sharp; skills smooth,
The first square snapped off
Quickly raised
And placed between eager lips.

The cast off skin skids along the street
Pleasure over -
But not forgotten.
The gentle taste lingers on, reminding
Indefinitely.

Helen Thorpe (15)
Sutton High School

The Summer

My pool is sparkling in the sun,
The summer light has just begun,
The petals that fall in the pool,
Give off a ripple that looks rather cool.

The hot sun starts to burn my face,
So I look inside my swimming case,
What I find is sunscreen so white,
I put it on, my face feels light.

Deeply, I plunge into the water,
Something grabs my foot and says, 'Caught ya,'
I jump with shock and turn around,
My brother's laughing face I found.

My little dog runs and jumps and barks,
While my brother and I swim like sharks,
We swim and swim to our hearts' delight,
But we end up having a big fight.

Even though winter isn't that bad,
When summer comes along, I'm glad!

Hannah Patrick (12)
Sutton High School

Problems

As they walked along the lane,
It suddenly began to rain.

But the girl had no hat!
And had hair as furry as a tabby cat!

Then as they continued to walk along,
The boy felt as shivery as a gong!

So they ran home, as fast as they could,
To get some straightness and a coat with a hood.

To stop the shivering and the frizz,
I hope it works or they'll be in such a tizz.

Maisie James (12)
Sutton High School

Bullies

They know exactly what they're going to do.
Even if they really don't want to.
No one understands what they're going through.
They may seem high up, but they're much lower than you.

They're insecure with themselves,
They're upset and going through Hell.
You would never be able to tell.
Because they're locked up inside a shell.

They're scared of something inside.
They have something they have to hide.
They take it out on people by being unkind.
But, they're all mixed up inside their mind.

You must think this is the victim.
For they get hurt too.
But no it is the bully.
Who is confused and has nothing better to do.

Karina Siba (14)
Sutton High School

I Will Keep Christmas

When you take a step outside,
It feels like a dream,
A wonderland of white winter snow.

You can see windows covered in icicles and frost,
Curtains are drawn but the firelight still shines through,
It is beautifully decorated inside.

This Christmas world is like Heaven,
The tree is covered in tinsel,
It glistens in the light from the candles of sweet silver fire.

Is this what we love about Christmas?

Catherine Branter (12)
Sutton High School

Mood Swings

I'm stressed, I'm stressed,
My hair is messed,
I don't know what to do.
I'm cross and moody,
Angry and broody,
And my life's all in a stew.

I'm happy, I'm happy,
I'm zippy, I'm zappy,
I'm so high I could touch the sky,
The energy is flowing,
It won't stop going
I keep jumping, shouting 'Oh my.'

With the depression I'm feeling,
It really is seeming,
That nothing will ever go right,
I feel so alone,
Numb as a stone,
Crying into the night.

I'm laughing, I'm smiling,
The schoolwork is piling,
I really can't manage to care,
Oh what joy,
I could never be coy,
I just want to dance in the air.

This time of the month,
I greet with a 'humph'
It's always affecting my mood,
One moment happy,
And then I'm snappy,
Then I just binge on the food.

Emma Inkester & Sarah Infante (16)
Sutton High School

Ahead Of The Wind

I sit in the saddle and gather up the reins,
Pale legs move underneath me,
The white man sitting on a golden neck,
My horse lifts her head and looks at what's ahead.

She's trotting then, faster and faster,
The mane lifts off her neck,
And her head stretches ahead; racing the wind,
The swishing grass stamped down beneath her hooves.

She lengthens her stride and looks up,
Then her forelegs snap up and we're flying,
Flying like a hawk, before we land again,
And are galloping towards the trees.

Eventually she slows down to a canter,
And then a trot, I urge her on,
But she is adamant, her mouth is foaming,
Steam rises from her flanks.

Harriet Trefusis (13)
Sutton High School

Autumn Leaves

How silently they tumble down
And come to rest upon the ground
To lay a carpet, rich and rare,
Beneath the trees without a care,
Content to sleep, their work well done,
Their colours gleaming in the sun.

At other times, they wildly fly
Until they nearly reach the sky.
Twisting, turning through the air
Till all the trees stand stark and bare.
Exhausted, drop to earth below
To wait, like children, for the snow.

Keerthana Nimaleswaran (12)
Sutton High School

Hallowe'en

Hallowe'en is already here,
Vampires, devils, all to fear,
The spooky games are so much fun,
The Hallowe'en night has just begun.

Trick or treating is daring and scary,
Knocking on people's doors you get so wary,
You even get scared of tiny mice,
But the candy tastes all so nice.

You walk along the street,
Different costumes that you meet,
Witches, angels, ghosts and bats,
Do you know who's inside that cat?

Walking home along the rustling trees,
You think you are as scared as can be,
But then you see a twisting shadow,
Who's that person in the meadow?

You start to run to eat that candy,
The road is smooth but also sandy.
The Hallowe'en night has come to an end,
I'll have to wait for it to come again.

Holly Ramsey (12)
Sutton High School

My Memory Poem

Oh cute, Mum, who is that,
The one with curly hair,
The one wearing the sweet red coat,
And the bonnet upon her head.

Oh yes Lucinda, a day I remember well,
The day my sister wed,
You are the girl with the sweet red coat,
And the bonnet upon your head.

Everyone said nice things,
About my little child,
Although on the day you had a cold,
A cold that was quite mild.

The weather didn't help it,
It made our noses run,
But even though this was the case,
We still had lots of fun.

The bride she looked so pretty,
In the dress that she was wearing,
No wonder all the passers-by,
Were standing still and staring.

Dearest love I will never forget you,
On the day my sister wed,
You were the one with the sweet red coat,
And the bonnet upon your head.

Lucinda Maria Vieira Martins (12)
Sutton High School

Kidnapped

I pass the shadow of tranquillity and exultation,
His grimace penetrating my feared eye,
I am sanguine but affected by menace,
My spirit has been diminished.

This is mere inhumanity,
Where tears of oppression and mystery haunt my face,
These tears will not wash away my pain,
Instead, evil of the past will shatter my soul.

Perpetual retribution is what I am experiencing,
Falling into the mysterious hands of unknown fingers,
I await more depression,
Impatiently listening out for encouraging words.

No consolation has been given to me,
But more intangible dangerous thoughts being perceived,
It is like a dream of savagery,
That lasts every brutal day and night.

I live through days full of peril,
Captured inside by suspicious figures,
Isolated between walls of gloom,
I try to fog my past memories.

My ruthless experiences echo in my mind,
I attempt to detach myself,
From this vivid mercilessness,
But I am fruitless.

I am restricted in whatever I do,
This depravity is stronger than my good-heartedness,
My courageousness is nil,
And so is my inside.

I continue to be devastated,
Shielded from goodness and hope,
I remain shattered,
And blank in virtue.

Victoria Hallam (13)
Sutton High School

The Way Of The Rainbow

It started on a Sunday,
And ended on a Monday,
This is how the legend began,
When the phone had rung,
It was Emily on the other end,
Telling me about her latest trends,
In the distance I could see,
A rainbow by the forest trees,
I told her maybe we could find,
The end of the rainbow if we used our minds,
Rewards we would get,
So off we set,
So went the rainbow search,
We went to look at the church,
It was nowhere to be seen,
But we were both still keen,
To the forest we thought,
It seemed the rainbow didn't want to be caught,
Next stop was the school,
Where we finally found it in the hall,
There was a large pot from what we could make out,
We were so excited we began to shout,
The whole pot was filled with gold,
Then Emily went ever so cold,
She had turned to me with an evil stare,
A look that called, mind out, beware,
She walked along the rainbow arch,
Up she went march by march,
She fell down a hole,
The rainbow said to have taken her soul!

Elise Dalman (12)
Sutton High School

The Mysterious Man

Whistling through the gravestones,
Like a current in the air,
It whips around his cracking bones,
And distresses his rugged hair.

The man standing in the doorway,
Amongst the shattered church walls,
The coarse grass sways around the bay,
It echoes as he calls.

His teeth are like rotting clothes pegs,
His dull eyes are sunken in,
While he scurries on two straggly legs,
He hunts towards the bins.

The gushing rain now thunders around him,
As he whistles a faint odd sound,
He creeps up towards a rusty bin,
And takes out some greasy chips,
Pleased in what he's found.

He now scrambles back to the gravestones,
And sits by a cold stone wall,
He yells at his aching bones,
As he rests to sleep until dawn.

Laura Hamer (13)
Sutton High School

My Enemy

I look in the mirror,
My worst nightmare,
My reality stares back at me,
The cheeks red and swollen,
The rolls of fat enveloping my body,
The clothes stretched on,
Straining at the seams,
The ten-year-old girl,
Her face pale and sad,
Her eyes downcast.

I step on the scales,
They plunge under my weight,
It's worse than last night,
Far worse,
I run from the room,
Tears stinging my eyes,
Until I find refuge,
Downstairs by the fridge,
To spend another night alone,
With my friend,
My enemy,
Food.

Sarah Willis (14)
Sutton High School

Fish

I'm not that keen on fish,
It's not my ideal dish,
There's a few I so dislike,
One of those is pike,
I have a strong hate,
For a revolting fish called skate,
I've never tasted sprat,
The smell put me off that,
I once ate a piece of carp,
But thought it was too sharp,
Before I have tried brill,
And that was not a thrill,
I did once try hake,
But that was a mistake,
I really cannot understand,
Why people like something so bland,
You can eat fishes big and small,
But I'm afraid to say I despise them all!

Camilla Barden (12)
Sutton High School

Autum Is Coming . . .

Autumn is coming
As the clouds
Hide behind the sky

Autumn is coming
No one, no one
Knows it.

The wind whispered to me
Trees and the sky
Will be darker

As autumn is coming . . .

Stephanie Yook (14)
Sutton High School

Hope

What is hope?
Is it something we can rely on in times of need,
Or will it stab you in the back and shatter
You into pieces when you're least expecting it?

Is hope worth believing in?
If we do believe in it, will it take all our fears
And troubles away
Or will it just increase them?

Hope is such a small word, yet
It can make so much difference in someone's life.

Hope makes you hide from the truth,
But it gives you strength and courage
To carry on in life.

Shaline Fazal (13)
Sutton High School

Then And Now

Meeting new people on our way,
Saying goodbye to those that couldn't stay.

Through the bad times and the good,
We have grown up as we should.

What started as a quarter,
Has ended as a whole.

Say goodbye to old friends,
And say hello to the new.

The last light has died,
And so it is time to say our goodbyes.

To those we have grown with,
And now wish we could stay with.

Taler Kelly (11)
Sutton High School

Castaway

Isolated, devastated,
Castaway on an island,
Calmness, stillness,
Surrounded by silence.

Away from other people,
Away from civilisation,
Away from wars and conflict,
Not part of any nation.

No commands or orders,
No rules to follow,
No laws and regulations,
No places in sorrow.

No one to comfort,
No one to talk to,
No one to laugh with,
And no one to cry with you.

Isolated, devastated,
Castaway on an island,
Loneliness, fearfulness,
Surrounded by silence.

Niamh Connaughton (13)
Sutton High School

Homeless

I'm tired and I'm hungry
And I'm dressed in rags,
I need food and a bed
But you pass me by.

I'm dirty and I'm poor
And I'm dressed in rags,
I need money and a wash
But you pass me by.

I'm calling and I'm begging
And I'm dressed in rags,
I need some love and care
But you pass me by.

I'm lonely and I'm friendless
And I'm dressed in rags,
I need a life of fun
But you pass me by.

I'm homeless and pathetic
And I'm dressed in rags,
I need help and a home
But you pass me by.

Esther Nicoll (14)
Sutton High School

Open Your Eyes

If you could see the future, what would you do?
Would you stop all wars
Or paint the sky blue
Or would you close all doors
And retreat into a shell,
Or would you open your eyes to the outside world?

If you could change the past, what would you change?
Would you just change your own life
Or would you change others as well?
Would you do the right thing, not always for you?
Would you do something wrong to make your family's life askew
And never open your eyes to the outside world.

Open your eyes and you will see things anew.
You can't see the future or past.
You should learn to be content and when you do,
You will have opened your eyes to the outside world.

Just open your eyes!

Elizabeth Main-Ian (12)
Sutton High School

School

I'm nervous.
What would it be like in high school?
How can I find out?

Would it be scary?
Would the teachers be so kind?
Now I have to find out if you mind.

High school is excellent!
I was right, the teachers are so kind,
Now, you have to find out what it's like.

Tharani Packiahrajah (11)
Sutton High School

The Four Seasons

Each new year begins in the middle of winter,
With snow, ice and biting winds.
The sun has no warmth; the air is cold and frosty,
The days are short and the nights are long.

The world bursts into bloom in spring,
With mad March winds and blustery April showers.
Blossom hangs heavy on the branches of the trees,
Whilst the birds are busy, building their nests.

Summer days are hot and lazy,
With picnics, barbecues, parties and fêtes.
Holidays are spent in far-flung places,
Everything is relaxed and fun.

Now comes autumn, with its brilliant colours.
The leaves are falling and the mornings are misty.
Bonfires glow in the fading light,
Winter soon returns with an icy blast.

Charlotte Howson (13)
Sutton High School

The Days Go Past

The days go past one by one,
No hope, no joy,
I'm just a boy,
All stuck and lonely, nowhere to go.

I've given up,
There's nothing left,
Just to wait,
Then run, I'm told run,
Escape, escape,
My journey has begun.

Fleur Godwin (11)
Sutton High School

A Cautionary Tale -
(This is why you must learn to swim. Read this tale and let it sink in)

A boy named John just would not swim,
Though it was very good for him.
He claimed the water was too cold,
And he was rather posh, I'm told.
The only water he'd accept
Was in his glass and in his bed.
A rubber pouch of quality,
Fit for the reigning monarchy
Would be filled till it was boiling
To enhance young Johnny's snoring
Until that fateful day arose
When little John lay in repose.
He squashed the pouch until it tore,
It burst, so drenched the bed and floor.
Poor Johnny cried out in alarm
As tsunamis broke his arm.
He screamed and bellowed till he choked.
As water filled his narrow throat.
He yelled out but to no avail,
So he drowned - that is my tale.

Sonia Tong (12)
Sutton High School

My Dog

My dog's name is Maya,
She slumps about all day long,
And she likes to play ping-pong.
She is very fat,
And likes to chase cats.
She doesn't run in a straight line,
But always follows the sign.
My dog is very lazy,
But she is very crazy.
She is mad about my dad,
And when he is gone she is sad.
She eats a variety of food,
But after she is in a bad mood.
She is as playful as a cat,
But as blind as a bat,
She messes about all the time,
But never commits a crime.
She is loving when you are feeling down,
Always manages to take off my frown
And that is why I love my dog!

Priyanka Amin (13)
Sutton High School

Autumn

Walking through the school grounds
Every manoeuvre I make.
I hear the crinkle, the crunch, of the leaves
Which swiftly fall to the ground.
The colours so rich of yellow, reds and browns,
All falling from the trees to leave them bare.

Looking around me all I see
Are little boys playing conkers
As happy as can be

As the children settle down to work
The school playground stands still
Suddenly the flicker of a silver fur
Darting from tree to tree
The naughty squirrels are out at play
Digging briskly to conceal their
Acorns, nuts and seeds.

Outside the school fence
The trees stand cold and bare
The warm sweet smell of roasting chestnuts
Hits the open air.

Karis Kennedy (12)
Sutton High School

Wounding Of The Soul

Boom!
Yet another bomb drops.
Ssss,
The evil hissing of poisonous gases
Wafts through the scorching air.

People fall gently to the ground,
Muffled moans,
Crucial cries,
Despair is everywhere in this dreamworld.

Silence falls,
Radioactive waves pass swiftly and silently
Through the desolate landscape, like a deadly killer.
Poverty and darkness enhance us.
Nothing is left.

Suddenly it dawns on us,
This dreamworld is reality.
Nowhere to run to,
Nowhere to hide.

Some moments stay with you forever.

Fiona Cooper (13)
Sutton High School

The Wounded Soldier

Duck!
She didn't see it in time
She got hit in the weakest spot
It was right on target
She was shivering from shock

Her eyes blinded
People rushing to her aid
The numbness she felt was indescribable
She lay back and tried to relax
Her hands stinging

She was dragged to safety
Behind the fort that was made
Her wounded body leaving a trail in the snow
She had still not said a word
We were worried

As we wiped her face
With the cleanest part of Sean's glove
We waited anxiously for a reply
Her face went sour and shook as she came to
She sat up and gasped

We assisted her, as she was weak
And looked at her frightened eyes
Her whole body shaking from the cold
She spat out remainders of snow in her mouth and said,
'That snowball got me right in the face!'

Santina Philips (14)
Sutton High School

Seal

See how he dives
From the rocks with a *zoom!*
See how he darts
Through his watery room.
Past crabs and eels
And green seaweed.
Past fluffs of sandy
Minnow feed!
See how he swims
With a swerve and a twist,
A flip of the flipper,
A flick of the wrist!
Quicksilver-quick,
Softer than spray,
Down he plunges
And sweeps away;
Before you can think,
Before you can utter
Words like, 'Dill pickle'
Or 'apple butter'
Back up he swims
Past stingray and shark.
Out with a *zoom!*
A whoop, a bark;
Before you can say
Whatever you wish,
He plops at your side
With a mouthful of fish!

Hasret Sayan (11)
Sutton High School

Mother Nature

She gingerly plasters a few wisps of hair behind one earlobe
Her hair is the shade of a moonless sky
Her eyes are piercing jewels

Her frail emaciated fingers wither in the harsh winds
She clasped her hands and slowly exhaled;
Clinging on to each and every breath as if it may be her last

She stands, the focal point of her surroundings
She is graceful like a white stallion among a herd of boars
Her beauty is as radiant as the glamorous sun

Each of her features is eminent
Her mouth; soft and luscious, like a comforting friend, always there for you
Her nose is elegantly defined, each line and kink perfectly composed

Her body is motionless and perfectly aligned
All that moves, is her eyelashes fluttering in the ruthless winds
She is a recluse, as passers-by stop to gaze long at her dazzling features

She will remain for generations to watch over us with pure tranquillity
She brings the first harmonious blossom each spring
She murders the very last flower of each summer

She transforms the leaves from emerald green to crimson, red, yellow
She is here to make the first glorious snowfall and to watch it disappear
Some call her a witch and some a miracle worker
But I call her, Mother Nature.

Sana Sheikh (13)
Sutton High School

Poem For Hallowe'en

Knock! Knock!
Who's that person knocking on my door?

Knock! Knock!
There is garlic hanging up next door.

What is making that scary sound?
A skeleton bug, rattling around.

Knock! Knock!
Who's waiting on your door?
Scary children in costumes I saw.

Knock! Knock!
Who's waiting on your door?
Children in groups of four.

Knock! Knock!
Who's waiting on your door?
Greedy children wanting more.

Knock! Knock!
Who's looking for you?
I don't have a single clue!

Knock! Knock!
Who's waiting on your door?
Open it if you dare, to see who's
waiting for you there.

Poh-Yee Wan (12)
Sutton High School

If Only

If I was Mum and Mum was me,
I'd already have my honours degree.

Her credit card would be my own,
I'd have long chats on her mobile phone.

I would drive really fast in her flashy sports car,
And stop off for a drink at the nearest bar.

I could watch any film and stay up really late,
I wouldn't have anyone watching what I ate.

I would wear stilettos nearly every day,
There would be no rules I'd *have* to obey.

But how would Mum cope at being me,
Could she survive double chemistry?

She'd find the homework hard to do,
With teenage slang she'd have no clue!

Going to bed early she'd find a pain,
Teenage spots she'd suffer again.

Her money would be in short supply,
Would she fall in love with every fit guy?

If Mum was me and I was Mum,
Life for me would be much more fun.

Hannah Nicoll (14)
Sutton High School

The Rainbow

Red like the colour of love, at first sight a shock
but at second a pleasure.
Orange the colour of warmth, fills you inside with joy.
Yellow, bright and cheerful like the sun, a symbol of happiness.
Green the colour of the leaves and grass,
nature's way of sharing its beauty.
Blue like the sky, peaceful and tranquil, a calming colour.
Indigo, the harsh effect of the shade touches you
somewhere deep down inside.
Violet, a joyful colour, it makes you feel fresh,
and as I look out of the window, I see the rain
pouring down harshly like tears streaming down an unhappy sky,
and the sun beaming down on us like the
happiness of the forgiving clouds.
And in the middle, the partition to both, I see
the solution, a long gleaming, beautiful, colourful
rainbow in all its glory.

Krupa H Thakker (12)
Sutton High School

Winter

Winter comes as a surprise,
It nips you like a bird,
Winter is a cold and dreary time,
It's a month that is as white as snow,
Winter is like a coconut,
Hard on the outside but soft in the middle,
Winter freezes everything,
The ground, your ears and your toes,
Winter can be rain, sleet or snow,
It varies all the time you know,
Winter can pounce,
It can catch you out when you least expect it,
Winter is not loved by many,
But others like it as spring follows on.

Sophie Penwarden (12)
Sutton High School

Grey

I counted the things in my room today,
All the things that were coloured grey,
And with nothing to do and with nothing to say,
I thought I'd do something about the grey.

I thought I'd paint my room too,
I tried to paint my room blue,
I said, 'I like this colour,
I'll stick to it like glue,'
But after moments I realised,
I didn't like the blue.

I tried the colours green and red,
But it looked just like mouldy bread,
I tried the colours black and white,
But that just didn't look right.

Then I saw why black and white
Just didn't really look right.
They had melted into one another,
And smothered each other like a mother.

So the items in my room are grey,
And it's always going to stay that way,
Until one day I say to grey,
'Be on your dark, dull way!'

Hannah Wastnidge (11)
Sutton High School

Family

Brothers are annoying,
They always want a fight.
Brothers like to hit you,
Or pinch you at first sight.

Sisters can be stroppy,
They never lend you shoes.
Sisters borrow T-shirts,
Which they tend to lose.

Mothers like things tidy,
Especially your room.
They always like things done on time
If not, you'll meet your doom.

Fathers watch the football,
Although they never win.
They always tend the garden,
And throw things in the bin.

They like to scream and shout at you,
They're annoying as can be.
Really they do love you,
They are your family.

Kathryn Griffiths (14)
Sutton High School

The Balloon

The balloon it flew
High as could be,
Its red rubber,
Shining with glee.

It bounced on the clouds,
It ran through the air,
It screamed over mountain tops,
Into the lion's lair.

The balloon flew out,
Drifting away,
Down and down
Then soaring through the day.

It soon got lower,
Was never going to stop,
But there was a pin,
And the balloon went *pop!*

Carla Busso (13)
Sutton High School

My Doom

They laugh at my glasses,
They laugh at my hair,
They laugh at my weight,
I pretend I don't care.

My friends take no notice,
They think it's a lie,
My parents don't know
They don't hear me cry.

They follow me home,
Calling me names,
It always happens,
Always the same.

I cry at home,
Alone in my room,
Dreading tomorrow,
Dreading the doom.

Josie Rawes (13)
Sutton High School

Stuck

Sitting in a classroom,
Wondering what to do,
The task; to write a poem,
On a subject that interests you.

Everyone around me,
Is scribbling down their feelings,
Using a thesaurus and dictionary,
Checking the spellings and meanings.

They're writing of worries and fears,
Based on books they have recently read,
About adventures in far-off places,
Of things other people have said.

My brain wasn't working today,
Now it's time to hand in our work,
But I haven't done anything at all,
Just written down the thoughts in my head,
But hey, it rhymes and is in verses!

I'm a poet
And I didn't know it!

Sarah Bishop (11)
Sutton High School

A Little White Stick
(Dedicated to my late Nanny Joy)

That little white stick,
goes into one's mouth,
damaging a body,
destroying the health.

Millions die each day,
from smoking, that's all,
a fatty, thick mess injected
yet still so small.

An awful habit you will see,
in newspaper messages that scare,
stories so tragic,
people can only stare.

That little white stick,
goes into one's mouth,
damaging a body,
destroying the health.

Laura Gillhespy (11)
Sutton High School

A Dream Come True?

As I was in geography, looking for Kentucky,
I wondered what would happen if I got lucky.
If I had the chance of being a superstar,
Imagine if I did go far.

On the catwalk I would always be,
With lots of fans, goodbye boring old me!
The main character in every play,
I could never rest all day.
Pestering paparazzi begging for a pose,
Every man I see would give me a rose.

But every girl needs her rest,
No more concerts, I must protest!
Geography is where I want to be,
I want to go back to boring old me!

Jessica Crowson (12)
Sutton High School

Famous . . .

Sitting at home watching TV,
Movies, music and telly for free,
Watching jealously, wanting to be . . .
Singing and acting wish they could see me,
All the clothes, make-up and hair,
Wish I was a star, so I didn't have to share,
Seeing famous people, acting, dancing and singing on TV,
I wish, I wish . . . that could be *me!*
All your talent and passion comes in for free,
when you get to be on air and TV,
All hard work on the shoots, you can't even
stand on your high heels or boots
If I was a star, I'd want to go back to the old me . . .
At home watching movies, music and telly, for free.

Asha Pankhania (12)
Sutton High School

Can We?

Can we love those who are mean, greedy and evil?
Have we any room in our hearts
To try to pardon those who cause pain and grief to others?
If we can learn to live with and forgive them,
We can make the world a better and safer place.

Can we help those who are poor, lonely and feeble?
Have we any care in our hearts?
If we try to give hope to those who are ill
And in grief and despair,
We will be a stronger and more grateful people.

Can we live in peace and tranquillity together as one?
Have we any inspiration and acceptance in one another?
If we can learn to tolerate and love,
We can find courage in each other and learn to respect who we are.
The Earth was made for us all to live in and enjoy,
Has it got many years left?
Only we can decide.

Natasha Patel (11)
Sutton High School

Pompeii

P ompeii's hot sun shone bright,
   as sweat dripped down my forehead,
O nly tragic thoughts went through my mind
   of the 24th August.
M emories I'd never lived through,
P eople's screams I'd never heard,
E ven the soot black ashes reminded me
   of the red hot lava I'd never seen.
I nterested people had a grin on their face,
I n the same place where nature had once stolen the lives of many.

Daisy Ukoko-Rongione (12)
Sutton High School

Autumn Queen

As the leaves fall gently onto the squashed carpet of mud,
As the wind blows the neat pile of leaves into desolation,
As the frequent cries of happy children die down,
She knows that it is time.

She leaves her cave that has been her source of strength,
Her hazel eyes are hard and her ruby lips are stiff,
She dances - light as air - through the woods of contempt,
To reach her throne of thorns and thistles.

The battering winds attack her fragile bones,
Her deep set eyes are hurting - but she wears a cloak of valour,
Her feet long to move but they are set in the stone of nature,
She must wait.

Her crystal tears are falling,
Her dainty hands are shaking,
Her golden hair is flowing like a train on a bridal gown,
Who is she? The Autumn Queen.

Sarah Daoud (12)
Sutton High School

Living

I never thought living was worth a lot
But I was wrong
In the camp you never saw one speck of sunlight

In the camp where it was dark and cold
Getting beaten every day and frightened of tomorrow
Seeing the guards smirk at you and their eyes full of evil
Enjoying every moment of hurting you, starving you, killing

But here outside in the world
I now understand what beauty means.
The sun is bright like a fire and warm like a blanket
And the smell of fresh air; so sweet
The flowers, one tiny bulb that no one is interested in but when it opens
Its face is the prettiest thing

I feel sorry for the people back at the camp
How they will die in darkness and never hear laughter of joy
In the world there are some bad people but some are not
For back at the camp with them is hell, but outside that fence
is a different place
A place Johannes calls Heaven.

Kimberley Bennett (11)
Sutton High School

Bonfire Night

The fire arose
like an animal awakened from the dead.

It twisted and turned,
writhing like a mass of evil.

It consumed the air
and belched out fumes, that left a lingering
mark on everything it came into contact with.

It spat out flecks of fire,
like an angry guard dog growling.

It raged fiercely
and grew into a mass of fear and danger.

Some children stared with faces of awe,
as the fire danced and crackled.

However the fire gradually died,
as it started to rain drops of life.

The fire screamed
and recoiled painfully.

The rain had conserved the evil
and the embers faded into the ash!

Jennifer Ferguson (12)
Sutton High School

They Are Coming

They are coming.
We are so afraid.
Will they catch us?
We must keep running.

The children are crying.
A great sorrow has come
Since they came,
But we must keep running.

We can't go on for much longer.
Then they will catch us.
There will be no mercy.
We must keep running.

They are here.
The end has come.
Now life and death has no boundaries.
We are all going to die.

But what is this?
They are stopping, turning back.
After all they have slain.
The sun is here,
But tomorrow night we will fear again.

Elizabeth Priestley (11)
Sutton High School

I Am David

Living in this awful place,
Behind the guards, who have no face,
Behind the barbed wired fence,
Behind the guns.

They may take away my will to live,
They may take my future,
They may have taken my parents,
But they will not take my name; David, which is and
                                  always will be me.

Each day goes by with the dreaded thought of death,
One wrong word, that's all it takes,
They easily pull the trigger,
Gone from the world, lost.

Otherwise you have to work,
Be their slave and be tortured,
With so little food to live on,
With little life worth living.

Siân-Louise Tangney (12)
Sutton High School

Down In The Jungle

Deep down into the jungle
Among the tall trees
There is a tall giraffe, who eats up all the leaves

If you go down further,
You might meet some buzzing bees,
But be careful you don't get stung - please!

There is a slithering snake
Who likes to drink from the lake
And apart from all the hissing, he likes to take a break.

Then nearby a lion growling
Next to it, a tiger prowling
But the animals won't come near
All except the great big bear.

But now to end the poem alas
The animals lie on the grass
When the birds stop tweeting
The jungle starts sleeping.

Natasha Batish (12)
Sutton High School

What Is It?

The walls are damp,
The walls are dreary,
I'm frightened that no one,
Will ever hear me.

If the walls could talk,
They'd tell me a story,
I bet you anything,
That it would be gory.

Oh no they've got me,
There's something on my head,
However will I go on?
I wish I was dead.

The stairs give a creak,
And my heart thumps loudly,
The lights flick on,
And my mum stands proudly.

Get back upstairs now,
And go back to bed,
And please, oh please,
Get that bowl off your head.

So off to bed I walked,
My head hung low,
Was it all just a dream?
We shall never know.

Kyndra Vorster (12)
Sutton High School

Winter Wonderland

Winter wonderland whisk me away
Away from the cold and away to play

Winter wonderland hear me sing
Sing the things that Christmas brings

Winter wonderland deep in my mind
To hear my thoughts that are wrong and kind

Winter wonderland feel my pain
The pain I have now and the pain I am to gain.

Winter wonderland leave me alone
Pack your things and go home

Winter wonderland you laughed at me
Go away and leave me be

Winter wonderland I hate you so
You don't love me so please go

Winter wonderland you were my friend
Our friendship has come to an end.

Elizabeth Egbe (12)
Sutton High School

Hallowe'en

A ghostly skeleton, what will come next,
A witch, a wizard, even some new pets?
But the scariest thing on Hallowe'en,
Is the oldest, mightiest pumpkin queen.
The sweets and candy the people share,
The bogie men and the monsters which scare.
Be very wary as the night draws near,
As the werewolves howl you should start to fear.
You hear a cry from the darkness and gloom,
A voice in your head, it's the voice of doom.
You run down the stairs and you see a face,
Are you in a different world or place?
The bright moon which gleams in front of your eyes,
It is like a present or a surprise.
The magic has faded, the night has passed,
The screaming and the shouts have gone at last.
This is the scariest night to be seen,
It's now all over - till next Hallowe'en.

Sarah Monger-Godfrey (12)
Sutton High School

My Cats

I've got six cats
Whom I like to pat
Two are orange, one is grey
One is multicoloured
And he doesn't like to play
One is black
They're always jumping up and down
Charlie is my favourite,
Because he's mine
He always comes to me
And we have a good time.

Shaun Allen (11)
The Park School

I Love Brainiac

I like to watch Brainiac
and I am a maniac.

Before every break on Brainiac,
I take part and guess in *'What's This?'*
And *'Which Fruit Floats?'*

In the Brainiac lab some people wear
white lab coats.

Another thing I like to take part in is
'Things John Tickle's Body Can't Do!'
I try to do what the nurse tells John Tickle to do, too!

Harry Milner (11)
The Park School

The Whale

One day I saw a whale
Just across the sea,
It was really far away
Over the horizon, happy as can be.

It was really loud, like a horn
And as dull as the night,
The air hole is an entrance to a tube
The top half is plain and white.

It is as powerful as the wind,
It is as slow as a snail,
It really takes its time,
I think it's a *whale!*

Thank you for reading
This whale poem,
It was really kind.
The ocean will keep flowing.

Luke Comley (13)
The Park School

Harvest Time

Everyone: Harvest Time By 8H

Aldo and Gary: Harvest time is the best time of the year
It is harvest time now

Joe and Marc: As we gather each and every ear
Of corn, we'll show you how.

Everyone: Red apples, blackberries, yellow berries too
The farmer gathers in the fruit for me and you

Jeremy & Blake: The leaves are falling off the trees
Time to grow some more

Ashleigh: The farmer gathers pods of peas
There are acorns on the floor

Everyone: Cabbage, cucumbers, tomatoes and Swede
Spinach, carrots, all things we need

Aldo: Everyone goes out to play
Throwing leaves every day
As the wind blows leaves everywhere
Dad comes out to clear away

Everyone: Red apples, blackberries, yellow berries too
The farmer gathers in the fruit for me and you

Gary: Adults gather the wheat to make flour and bread
Boys and girls collect conkers instead

Joe: More leaves are falling off the trees
More acorns are falling
More fruit is being gathered in

Everyone: Cabbages, cucumbers, tomatoes and Swede
Spinach, carrots, all things we need

Jeremy: We grow them all from seed
The enjoyment of the food we eat
It gives us all a treat
Harvest colours, red, yellow, brown and green
What a sight to be seen
Golden sun to ripen the fruits
And make our faces gleam

Everyone:	Red apples, blackberries, yellow berries too The farmer gathers in the fruit for me and you
Blake:	Conkers are falling onto the ground For children to play their game Autumn is with us So winter is on its way
Everyone:	Cabbages, cucumbers, tomatoes and swede Spinach, carrots, all things we need
Ashleigh:	These are all the things we need To help us grow big and strong We all start as little seeds And want to stay healthy for long
	The farmers set out their equipment and tools To harvest the crops before it's too cool
Everyone:	Red apples, blackberries, yellow berries too The farmer gathers in the fruit for me and you Cabbages, cucumbers, tomatoes and Swede Spinach, carrots, all things we need.

The Class of 8H
The Park School

School

S chool is fun
C lasses are hard
H arvest festival was great
O n the field, I play football
O n the playground I play
L unch is nice

I like
S cience

F rench will be difficult
U nless I try harder and
N ot butt in!

Connor Hobbs (11)
The Park School

Autumn

There are orange leaves in the autumn day,
Red leaves on a sunny day.

Yellow leaves and brown leaves,

The tree's leaves are changing red, yellow, orange, brown.
The trees are bare with no leaves
No leaves left to fall on the ground.

Luke Collier (13)
The Park School

Autumn

Every morning the sun gets up later
Showing the dew-laden lawns
Every morning the birds sing less
And I find it harder to wake

Falling leaves paint the streets
Twenty shades of brown
Formed into piles by the icy wind
For small children to kick around

Squirrels scamper, looking for food
Preparing themselves for winter
Competing with rosy-cheeked schoolboys
To find a prize-winning conker

Watching through steamy windows
As misty mornings turn into foggy nights
Hoping for a clear, bright day to see
The beautiful colours of autumn

The smell of bonfires fills the air
The quiet and dark of an autumn night
Broken only by a burst of fireworks
Then quickly falling back into silence and darkness.

Ryan Daily (11)
Wallington County Grammar School

My Adventure In Space

I had a weird dream that I was drifting in space,
But at first I didn't know it was this place.
Everywhere I looked was darker than night,
But there was an abundance of stars, they looked so bright.

The place was so grimly silent
It felt like my lifetime was totally spent.
I really didn't feel so scared
I would be interested to see how other people could have faired.

Suddenly what I saw made me fear,
An asteroid was pursuing me from the rear.
I turned around and what I saw
Was truly frightening, right down to the core.
The huge rock, bigger than the moon,
Was on a collision course with me, it was like a cartoon.

I tried to move with no time to spare
But I couldn't, I was stuck in the middle of nowhere.
I desperately struggled, I was slower than a snail,
It looked like the rock was going to prevail.

I started thinking I was about to die,
I thought that the end of my life was nigh.
The asteroid was approaching at speed, I couldn't beat it
I was stuck, I couldn't defeat it.

I then felt something grab my wrist,
It clenched so tight my hand turned into a fist.
My arms and legs were all over the place
It was like I was dangling from a rocket in a race.

It abruptly let go and I fell to the ground,
Then something fell on my head, it weighed something like a pound.
I opened my eyes and was on my head
The next thing I realised, I was off my bed!

Ishan de Silva (11)
Wallington County Grammar School

Rhythm

Starts with a rhythm
Soft on the snare
Bass drum beats
Bass drum beats

Think what I'm doing
Play a good fill
Crash on the cymbals
Go again, go again

Bass drum beats
You can't get the rhythm
When your feet 're like lead
You've got to get the feeling
Get the rhythm in your head
Bass drum beats
Bass drum beats

Body gets going
And the arms lift high
Feet get thumping
And the drumsticks fly
The air starts shakin'
And the wall's vibratin'
And the whole street's wakin' it,
takin' it, fakin' it,
Everybody's takin' it,
rakin' it, shakin' it
Now we're really makin' it!
Rhythm's really liftin' us,
shiftin' us, giftin' us.
Now we've got the rhythm in our head!

Josh Beer (12)
Wallington County Grammar School

The Dark And The Light

The light filled up the room,
Wiping out all the dark.
Leaving only grey shadows
Ignoring the light,
Ignoring the light.

The light bulb flickered on,
Letting no dark live.
Only the innocent were
Surviving the light
Surviving the light.

The light blasted away the darkness
Leaving no dark in the room.
The light spread out happiness.
The unhappiness was gone,
The unhappiness was gone.

The time had come to go to bed,
'No!' said the light.
Down went the light.
Happiness was gone,
Happiness was gone.

The darkness poured back in the room,
Leading all happiness into the stars.
The moon and all lights fought the dark,
The unhappiness was back,
The unhappiness was back.

The battle continued,
Light had beaten the dark.
The beautiful morning sun had risen,
Happiness had won,
Happiness had won.

Christopher Mann (11)
Wallington County Grammar School

The Image

I saw him lie there,
His agile body glistened through the night sky.
His feathers so tangled and messed,
He spread his vast wings
So crumbled and scoured.
He raised his face,
He opened his eyes of fire.
'Skellig!' I shouted.
He grinned his evil grin.

He took a small step
Then a few more, soon he was galloping.
He leapt . . .
His powerful body so streamlined,
Whilst soaring in the night sky.
He was the image.

Aravind Mootien (11)
Wallington County Grammar School

Skellig

I saw his face, dry and cracked,
Lumps protruded from his back
Like wings, folded under his coat.
His bird-like bones riddled with arthritis,
Creaked under the weight of his skin.
He stared back at me
With fearful eyes.
He sighed and asked for food.
'Food of the gods!' he craved.
Sliding back into the dust
Like a creature afraid of sunlight.
He curled up into the corner
And dreamt of taking flight.

Harry Pike (11)
Wallington County Grammar School

My Friends

The mornings can be terrible
This makes me very glum,
The workload can be terrible
This makes me very glum.

My school is most enjoyable
Because of all my friends,
I can get through the school day
Because of all my friends.

When the class is naughty
My friends and I feel sick,
When we're getting shouted at
My friends and I feel sick.

When I'm thinking about it
I'm so lucky to have my friends,
I know one thing for sure
I'm so lucky to have my friends.

Robert Maguire (11)
Wallington County Grammar School

School

When I wake up on a Monday morning, I realise that it's school,
My bag is packed from the night before,
Strapped to my back as I walk out the door
To Wallington school, who could want more?

I do lots of things in the school day,
Such as art, maths and my favourite play,
A delightful thing is my lunch,
In which all I do is munch and munch.

But I know too well that everything ends,
As I catch the bus home with some of my friends,
Strolling down the street to myself, I sing,
Going to school is a wonderful thing.

George Tully (12)
Wallington County Grammar School

School Life

As I walk through the year 8 playground,
I can see them playing football, shouting, playing and happy.
Then I reach year 7 playground
All my friends are playing and
Having a good time.
The sixth formers are telling everyone to line up,
Back to lessons I go.
I am meandering like a small river around other pupils,
Racing so that I won't miss my lesson,
Must make a good impression,
It's the same for every lesson.
When I reach the classroom I line up,
Silently until I'm asked to enter,
That's when we walk into the classroom silently
As if we had tape over our mouths.
We begin to unpack our heavy loads of books and our pencil cases,
We're told to sit down.
The lesson begins
At the end of each lesson, I hear the bell ring.
I start to pack away quickly, quietly,
To repeat the whole process again and again.
But however hard it is
I wouldn't swap it for being at home, at all.

Tom Kindler (12)
Wallington County Grammar School

The Point Of No Return

The sheer drop was in front of me,
The only way
Was down.
Into the fires of Hell,
The heat was burning.

A gust of wind blew in my eyes,
Blowing me backwards
In time.
My life flashed before my eyes,
All the bad associations eating
At my heart.

But then to my mind
Came my childhood
Happiness.
My mind was changing, against
My death

My mind was changing,
Twisting and turning.
I stumbled back,
I had chosen to live.

Edward Stedman (11)
Wallington County Grammar School

Death

It takes what it has given,
It wants a borrowed gift back.
It gives a reward if you use the gift of life correctly,
But gives eternal suffering if used incorrectly.

It gives an opportunity to rest before the trial of life,
And if passed, the greatest gift of all will be given.
It is the future for everyone,
And the goal for everyone to achieve.

When it lends the gift,
It gives a countdown before the true gift is given, not lent.
Men think of death as a black figure with a scythe,
But it is in fact the greatest of all God's servants,
As it can take you to the creator of the gift.

Life is a scale with good and evil balanced at the beginning,
Throughout the gift it outweighs both sides and gives a verdict.
If at the end it outweighs on the right side then you will meet your goal
But if it out weighs to the left, then your end will come.

Men should not fear the angel,
But should instead, embrace it.
If you fear it, the reason of fear will happen,
If you embrace it, you will also embrace God.

If you don't know evil,
Then you don't know righteousness.
If you don't know death,
Then you don't know life.

Without the gift then you would not know what the gift is
And without the gift you would not know what death is.
There is only life,
If it is taken.

Andrew Walsh (12)
Wallington County Grammar School

Race On

The qualifying begins,
Who will have pole?
Will anyone get a lap record?
The drivers begin to flow out,
The anxiety kicks in.

On to race day!
The engines begin to roar,
Teams leave the area,
All the spectators gaze over,
Everyone sits ready for the start.

Three, two, one, *go!*
Off goes the field.
Everyone looks in amazement,
Will anyone crash?
Who will win?

They all dive into the pits,
The mechanics get to work.
Who will be out first?
Will there be a new leader?
The teams begin to relax.

They begin the last lap,
Will there be a sudden change?
The leaders turn the bend,
They drive, side by side.
The chequered flag is shown
The winner is delighted
A race is completed.

Luke Davis (11)
Wallington County Grammar School

Music

Some people say that music is rubbish these days,
But I happen to love it.
Beats and rhythms beyond imagination
Lyrics combined by pure genius.

DJs taming the turn-tables and synthesisers,
MCs thoughtlessly chanting away at unknown speeds.
Rock stars smashing their vibrant, blaspheming guitars.
R 'n' B vocalists sing in unchained, harmonious melody,
Hip-Hoppers and rappers not just hitting the charts.
People nodding their heads to catchy tunes and
Mobile phones continuously playing ringtones like
                                  there's no tomorrow!

When people say that music is rubbish these days . . .
I say I'm loving it.

Michael Giblin-Burnham (12)
Wallington County Grammar School

The Evil Of Food

Why is food?
It starves, it overfeeds.
Why is food?
You're too thin and weak, you're too fat to move.
Why is bullying?
'Look at fatty! Ha ha! Ate too much!'
'It's a beanpole! Were you a twig in a past life? Ha ha!'
Why is hyper activity?
Pump me full of E-additives and partially inverted mega-glucose,
Sugar supplements with fluoromethydrocarbonrubunaniumtridite.
Why is heart problems?
Fat seizing your arteries in its epic quest to kill you.
Why is starvation?
Ethiopia is dying, yet we worship our gods, MacDonald's.
Are you 'lovin' it?'

Lewis Chaplin (12)
Wallington County Grammar School

Snow

I gazed out through the window,
White bits of rain were falling.
The purest of white it was
Landing on the rooftops.

They sparkled like diamonds bright,
Almost like angels' teardrops.
My sight was cold, a light blue,
But my soul was warm and soft.

'Snow!' My friends shouted with joy,
As they came to my window.
'Break's almost over!' they yelled,
Oh why were we not good?

The bell struck sadness in them,
A rush of sighs came all round.
Why were they in? They wondered
When all were having fun.

Thomas Lines (12)
Wallington County Grammar School

Death

As black as night
As cold as stone
More terrifying than the unknown
More sadder than being alone

As you see the numb body
Staring straight at you
There is a feeling you can't describe
As a shroud of fear overcomes you

Soon the sadness will drip away
But the wounds will never heal.

Simon Preston (11)
Wallington County Grammar School

There's An Awful Lot Of Weirdos In My Family
(Based on 'There's an awful lot of weirdos in our Neighbourhood' by Colin McNaughton)

There's an awful lot of weirdos
In my family!
Heck, too many weirdos
In my family.

For starters there's
My grandma,
Who says pasta like
It rhymes with plaster.

There's an awful lot of weirdos
In my family.

And I know
This physical mess,
Who's always
In a stress.

There's an awful lot of weirdos
In my family.

And my sister who
Sniffs a rag doll
That's called
Boo!

There's an awful lot of weirdos
In my family.

And finally my dad,
The only one
I thought was sane
Until he married Mum . . .

So, the only one who's totally sane
Would, of course, be me.

Adam Taylor (11)
Wallington County Grammar School

Two On One? Hardly Fair!

The brave soldier, there he stood,
The last of an epic army.

The battle-worn armour gleams,
The tunnelling eye socket.
The arm, merely a stump,
All hanging off the rotting carcass.

The tar coated teeth,
In a menacing grin,
The flashing blade
Waiting to be drawn.

The hand draws closer,
The sword leaves the sheath,
The mighty muscle swings the blade.
Not aimed at me but at the great bird.

The great eagle swoops down,
Thrusts its talons into the man's head.
The man is dragged off squirming and squealing.

The second man in the white sailor's hat,
Looked quite friendly at first,
When I saw the vicious bayonet.
It told me today might be my last.

His trigger finger itching,
I step back.
He steps forward,
I turn on my heels
He gives chase.

I climb a tree over a swamp,
Holding on for all I'm worth,
The ooze below splodges as the man steps in,
Sorry for him, the crocs were hungry!

Joe Henderson (11)
Wallington County Grammar School

The Race

I stood there on the line,
My muscles tight as a string bow,
Boys glanced, their faces full of determination
Which drilled through my ribs as my eyes widened.

The gunshot fired, which deafened my eardrums,
The race had begun but I set off at the back.
My arms propelled like a helicopter's blades,
Pushing my body and burning tendons, harder and harder.

I finally reached the last part of my journey,
I was drenched by the biting wind.
Blood pumped my muscles to a burning desire,
I had managed to pull myself up to second place!

Strength and stamina came from nowhere,
My sinews were lean and tight.
I intended to win the gold, whatever,
As I crashed through the ropes in style!

Daniel Heffernan (11)
Wallington County Grammar School

Skellig

Dust sprinkled from the roof,
Like raindrops from the skies.
He lay there, staring at nothing,
With his colourless but tender eyes.
I stood there trembling, terrified, afraid,
For he was terribly white and thin.
And included with rubbish that was littered around,
There were also small balls of skin.
With his squeaky voice, he spoke to me
His lips as dry as clay.
I stood there for a moment, looked, stared
Then I turned and ran away.

Calum Gordon (11)
Wallington County Grammar School

The Mystery Man

I went in the garage, I saw him there
At that moment he gave a mysterious glare

He stayed there waiting just to die
Each time I saw him I wanted to cry

I persuaded him to leave, he wanted to stay
I never knew he could fly away

In the new building he climbed up high
When we went near him our ghostly wings would fly

The baby was to die, he saved her heart
He was to fly from the dark!

The baby lives, her name is Joy
And that is what she brings us, for evermore.

James Brignull (11)
Wallington County Grammar School

Coal

As hard as rock
As black as night
When set alight
Will burn yellow, red and orange

Smoke rising from the flame
Air blackening
But coal burning strong
Like an eternal flame

As I gaze at the flame
I recoil as the heat starts to burn my skin

But now the fire is out
All that remains is the burnt coal
And the singed ground.

Ben McLellan (11)
Wallington County Grammar School

Alone In The Woods

I sit on a bench
Alone.
The darkness enveloping me
Like a huge black monster,
As the darkness creeps in on me.
I feel tired, worried, scared,
I feel tired but I can't fall asleep.
It's like I'm chained to a tree
I'm scared stiff.
I can't move an inch,
I want to run,
Be in bed or sit by the fire.
I can only wish that someone
Would come and help me.
I hear noises,
Howling,
Footsteps,
All from my imagination,
But they seemed so real.
Then I realise that they are real!
I turn,
I look,
I see
A scary black figure.
It takes one big leap and . . .
I wake up in bed.
I see it again, the scary black figure,
But this time for real.

Patrick Chea (11)
Wallington County Grammar School

Trip To China

I didn't take a slow boat to China;
I soared through clouds by jet plane,
Bumped and jostled down the runway
Towards the gleaming, glassy space-age terminal.
The heat struck my tired body
And jolted me back to wakefulness.
Spicy smells hung in the air
Inviting me to feast in this new world.
Hugged into the comfort of family, warm and welcoming
Smiling faces greeted me, eyes talking.
Speeding down the expressway, manic traffic,
Neon lights flashing from swanky skyscrapers.
Pagodas and poverty swept aside
Western culture invading the East.
Glimpses of the old;
Joss sticks on Grandmother's hillside grave.
Rickshaws, wrinkled beggars, bicycles,
Courtyard homes, carved wood chairs, jade, shrines.
Now my modern China calling;
Marble palaces and crystal chandeliers,
Construction sites, motorbikes, trucks and cars
Rushing into the future.
Chinese take-away, MacDonald's, Pizza Hut, KFC,
Chopsticks and crackling suckling pig,
Noodles and endless dim sum spinning round,
Comfort food of centuries.
I didn't take a slow boat to China
But I took the slow route home.

Calum George (11)
Wallington County Grammar School

Abducted By Aliens

When Rishi came back to school
After one day's absence, unexplained.
He went and told his teacher
He'd been abducted by aliens,
She told him not to be so daft
But he gave us all the details -
What the spacecraft had looked like,
How extra-terrestrials had kidnapped him,
Then carried him onto their ship.
And Rishi told his story,
Again and again!
'When they landed,' he said,
'I was terrified, I couldn't move,
I nearly died. Then a blade of light
Cut the night in two, and trapped me
In its beam so I couldn't see.
I felt arms that were wrapped around me
Like the coils of our garden hose.
And I don't recall anything more -
Except for being in an intergalactic laboratory!'

Rishi Bakrania (11)
Wallington County Grammar School

The Sabre-Toothed Tiger

Deadly figure
Death trigger
Silent walker
Blood stalker
Flesh ripper
Skin stripper
Arsenal jaw
Animal war.

Adam Lyons (11)
Wallington County Grammar School

Friend Or Foe?

The warmth-bringer is in my house today,
His home is black, black as night.
He brings safety but danger to all near,
But is a friend to most and heats their hearts.

His laugh is a crackle and spark,
He talks in a hiss and a splutter.
He playfully dances round the logs,
And teases the coal enveloped in his cloak.

His breath is a cloud of dark smoke,
It rises up into the heavens and disappears.
He's beautiful to a trained eye,
Full of colours, vibrant and bold.

But now he's dying, his spirit has gone,
He leaves behind a sullen ash.
He's cold, quiet and weak now
But in truth, he's sleeping until his return.

Joseph Williamson (11)
Wallington County Grammar School

School Poem

Finally school is over,
It felt like a million years,
I thought it would never end,
But what makes school worth going to?

English is exciting,
I hope Mrs Devereux teaches us more about writing
Classical is very interesting,
It makes me sad to hear the bell ring.

I love ICT, I wish there was more,
I hate that school law, I demand *more!*
Overall assembly is the best,
Learning new things can never be missed.

Shatik Patel (11)
Wallington County Grammar School

Skellig, Skellig

Skellig, Skellig what could he be,
A Devil, angel or a bat?
Skellig, Skellig sitting in the shed,
Sleeping at night on the floor, not a bed.
Skellig, Skellig must have been in pain
All the time, over and over again!

Skellig, Skellig young or old,
Skellig, Skellig thick or bold.
Skellig, Skellig how long did he rot -
Did he rot maybe, maybe not?

Skellig, Skellig did he help the baby,
Maybe! Just maybe, maybe!
Skellig, Skellig, where did he fly?
No one knows, maybe he'll just die!

Ben Donelien (11)
Wallington County Grammar School

The Whining Instrument

Lying fast asleep in its nice warm box
Was a trombone as gold as Goldilock's locks
A human picks it up, shining,
As the human blows, the trombone started whining.

It said, 'Now you listen to me,
You can only blow me if you have the key.'
The human was sad.

The trombone went back to sleep
A sleep which was deep
And he was *never*
>*used*
>>*again!*

Stuart Eldridge (11)
Wallington County Grammar School

In My Sleep

I saw it in my *sleep*
Not a *wink* did I sleep that day.
Its face was *pale* and ghastly
And his hair a *whitish-grey*.

I saw it in my *sleep*,
Not a *wink* did I sleep that day.
Its lips were thin and *crooked*
And its *breath* smelled of decay.

I saw it in my *sleep*,
Not a *wink* did I sleep that day.
Its eyes were cold and *lonely*,
And he *looked* at me in dismay.

I saw it in my *sleep*
Not a *wink* did I sleep that day.
Great wings spread from his shoulders,
I will *never* look at it in the same way.

Kwaku Dapaah-Danquah (11)
Wallington County Grammar School

Skellig

Skellig you make me *cry*
But now I know I have to say *bye!*
I see *your* wings
You want to *fly*.
Skellig, I *have* to say bye.
Will I see you again *before* I die?
Your *wispy-white* cheeks
Your *pale* white hips.
You saved *my* sister,
With your sips . . . *of beer.*

Adam Cousins (12)
Wallington County Grammar School

My Day

Sitting on the bus to school,
Thinking of my lesson plan,

Great, French first.
Oh no! I forgot
To learn my être verb.

Good, chemistry's next,
I like that a lot,
Using Bunsen burners.

Maths, brilliant!
As long as it is not
Multiples or algebra.

Then music. Ace!
I like Mrs Mott,
But not when we do singing.

Last thing, physics,
With results to plot.
Ah, I've broken my ruler.

Well, there's always lunch,
I'll have something hot.
Oh, I've lost my money!

Timothy McKavanagh (11)
Wallington County Grammar School

My View
(Based on 'Skellig' by David Almond)

I gazed at him through my eyes,
My woeful self entwined with lies,
In the dark I never sleep
My witful self forced to weep.

27 and 53 is what he brings,
Then runs back to his lodgings.
In the dark, did I sleep?
For tonight I do not weep.

Then there's a girl who tags along,
She talks of William Blake, his poems in song.
For tonight I also slept
But still I have not wept.

Wings come out I'm fit again,
The old me has been slain.
In the night I didn't sleep
In the hospital, did I creep?

The baby is safe yet again,
I said thank you to him for relieving my pain.
In the night I did not cry
Through the sky is where I fly.

Edward Butler (11)
Wallington County Grammar School

Angels

Faces look down at me
I have sleepless nights.
I know something's coming
It fills me with fright.

I want to go home,
To feel the same love.
Someone's up there
Looking from above.

The day has finally come,
It will decide my fate.
I hope they can do something,
I have a feeling it's just too late.

Hope spreads through me,
It's stronger than ever.
I'm soaring through the sky
As light as a feather.

It's all over now,
I feel extremely strong.
As long as I have hope,
Nothing will go wrong.

Crowds of smiling faces,
They look down at me,
I can feel my heart beating,
It's filled with joy and glee.

Angel that looked over me,
My many thanks go to you.
I know you'll always be there,
Flying through skies; truly blue.

Adib Chowdhury (11)
Wallington County Grammar School

Guilty

Worried
Scared
Guilty
The hardest feeling known to man

Trembling towards the Magistrate
Shaking like I'm cold
Scared
Feeling like never before

I start to sob
Like I am heartbroken
My fate in her hands
I can do nothing
I'm powerless to stop her

The decision is made
My heartbeat pumps heavily
Would it be
Prison?

The iron doors slammed in my mind
Fear ran through me
Standing still I wondered
Why?

Shocked and distraught
Walking off to prison
Crying uncontrollably
Shaking with fear

The verdict: *Guilty!*

Samuel Chislett (11)
Wallington County Grammar School

Skellig

Skellig, Skellig, how can you *live* like this?
In a *garage* like this,
Like a *skip*,
Full of *rubbish*.

You look so *weak*,
As thin as a *twig*.
Ready to *snap*
With a *gust* of the wind.

Your hair looks *greasy*,
As if it's never been *washed*,
It's *sleek* and black
Shining from the *light*.

Your clothes look *battered*,
Your skin looks *grubby*,
The eyes on your face look *dull*
And *not bright*.

However do you *live* like this?

Shane Freemantle (11)
Wallington County Grammar School

Skellig

He was half man and half bird,
Entwined in shadow,
Engulfed in mystery,
Trapped for eternity.

Then they gave him a chance,
That boy and that girl,
To escape from the duo of Arthur and Itis,
So he took his chance and flew, flew away,
To where he will be happy for the rest of his days.

Daniel Heronneau (11)
Wallington County Grammar School

Starting A New School

I walk in, everyone glares,
The giants push past, squashing me
I feel upset, alone.
To start all over again,
To start from the beginning.
The thought scares me,
They push past me again;
I am nothing to them,
Nothing to anybody.
Or am I?
I should be proud of who I am,
Proud to have withstood all I have encountered,
And I am proud now
Confident too.
This is not so bad
I'm pleased to be here.

Adam Gye (12)
Wallington County Grammar School

School

I wake up in the morning and I brush my teeth
What's the time? 7.30am!
Hurry up or I'm going to be late.
I get changed
Get into the car
And off we go.
I look in my contact book and what do we have?
Biology, English
And certainly games.
PSE, physics
The end of the day
The 410 is up on the way.
It's over now and I have a few words to say . . .
Good day.

Adam Makumbi (12)
Wallington County Grammar School

Another Day At School

We all arrive early in the morning,
To talk and play with our mates,
Interrupted by teachers and our lessons.
There goes the bell!
Off to registration, lessons begin.

Once again the bell has rung
For break to start.
Everyone runs through the corridors
To take part in the merriment.
The game has finished and lessons again.

Now onto rugby
Which is exciting,
No one stops or scores.
The bell has rung once again,
People throw their kit into their bags.

The bell has rung
We charge into the dining room,
Scoff the food down
So the game begins.
It's stopped by the teachers again.

The last lesson of the day,
Staring at our watches
Listening for the bell.
There it is - home time
We've gone in a flash.

Nihar Majmudar (11)
Wallington County Grammar School

School

At 7.05 I leave the house
To catch the 463;
I say goodbye to my pet mouse -
I'm as eager as can be.

I get to school early,
So as not to be late.
I say hello to all my friends
When reaching the school gate.

Hooray! Hooray! It's lunchtime,
And it will always rule.
I sometimes go to the canteen
To fill my tank with fuel.

My three top tips for secondary school
Are think, look and listen.
If you do these three things
At school, you'll really glisten.

I thought the teachers would be scary,
But the teachers are very kind.
I'm telling the truth, I really am,
No, I'm not out of my mind!

The bell has gone,
So home we go.
Tonight I've got some homework -
Oh no! Oh no! Oh no!

Thomas Wainford (12)
Wallington County Grammar School

Maybe I Should Foot It?

I *shall* foot it
Down the roadway, in the dusk.
Where shapes of hunger wander
And the fugitives of pain go by.
I *shall* foot it
In the silence of the morning.
See the night slur into dawn,
Hear the slow great winds arise
Where tall trees flank the way
And shoulder towards the sky.
The broken boulders by the road
Will not do anything to my ruin.
Regret will be the gravel underfoot.
I *shall* watch for . . .
Slim birds, swift of wing
That go where wind and ranks of thunder.
Drive the wild storms of rain.
The dust of the travelled road
Shall touch my hands and face.

Ciaran Alli (11)
Wallington County Grammar School

School Dinners

The dinners at my primary school
were tasteless and yuck,
The presentation was not great,
a daily plate of muck.
But now I'm at Wallington Boys'
the dinners are a treat.
Especially the pizza with pepperoni meat.

Thomas Housden (11)
Wallington County Grammar School

My Story

Entwined with beauty,
The gift of life.
Doubled hearts with my brother,
My forever other.
My heart was operated,
But now it's fine.
Proves I am just divine.

Courage was proven,
Pain was taken.
My brother,
Was horribly mistaken.

I've shown the will,
I've shown the fight.
Now I will have no sleepless nights.

Now I'm here,
I'll never leave,
Just got to breathe, breathe, breathe.

Benjamin Richardson (11)
Wallington County Grammar School

Happiness

Happiness is blue like a clear sky
It tastes like a refreshing cold drink on a hot day
It smells like freshly picked daffodils
it looks like a sunset, slowly fading away
It sounds like a soft stroke of a harp
It feels like a soft, fluffy and feathery pillow.

Christopher Jackson (12)
Wallington County Grammar School

The Storm

The sky begins to turn as black as
Coal,
The wind starts to
Whistle,
The rain begins to fall in
Showers,
And a storm makes its way
Overhead.
Thunder, lightning all around me, it is
Frightening,
I look at the storm and
Tremble,
It sends shivers down my
Spine.
The wind howls through the cold, night
Sky,
The rain crashes on the
Rooftops,
The thunder loudly rumbles over my
Head,
The lightning lights up the sky like a brilliant
Firework.
Then gradually the storm fades
Away,
As suddenly as it started it now
Stops.

Joshua Bell (11)
Wallington County Grammar School

Stairway To Heaven

Knock at my door
I'm always home
Alone

The door will open
A black hood will appear
Death

Come inside
But don't look back
Behind

Lie down upstairs
And close your eyes
Goodnight

I won't wake you in the morning
Have a lie in
Forever

Walk up the stairs
And through the clouds
With me

If you look back
Before the top
You'll fall

To flames
And hunger
Hell.

Jonathan Ganz (11)
Wallington County Grammar School

Seasons

S unrise appearing earlier, visible in the distance across
  dewy meadows,
P laying in the sunshine, a little warmer each day,
R elishing the hopeful thoughts of long hot summer days to come.
I n gardens, farms, cities and towns
N ew flowers, new leaves, new life, newness everywhere.
G rass springing up more luscious each hour, heralding brighter days

S un blazing on my back and cloudless skies fill me with joy,
U nderneath leaf laden trees, picnickers enjoy life outdoors.
M arigolds their delicate golden petals glisten far off
  in colourful fields,
M elting ice creams, dripping down soggy crumbling cones.
E asy, lazy sunny days, relaxing by cool waters.
R acing, happy children, their laughter ringing through the stillness.

A ll the glorious colours, red, yellow, orange and golden brown,
U mbrellas hunted for after the rainless summer.
T rees and their leaves parting company,
U mpteen conkers, nuts and acorns scattered on the barren ground.
M isty miserable mornings, cold, grey foggy days,
N early time for winter.

W et, ice-cold sleet and hail, rain down from above,
I n the moonlight, snow covered trees and hills glitter in the night
N othing can match the Yuletide anticipation of young and old
T hen toys discarded after happy festive days.
E ating steaming roast dinners radiating warmth within me.
R oaring wind, blowing cold but making me excited.

Michael Peter Brockman (11)
Wallington County Grammar School

Prometheus

The start of my story, as it's always told
Was when I pitied the humans, down there in the cold.
Both the ice and wild animals were biting,
Often the humans were losing the fighting.
Huddling in damp caves, keeping together
Their morale was low, whatever the weather.
Fire was what they needed to warm them
I made them, so had no reason to harm them.

Only we gods are allowed to have fire
We kept to this rule in fear of Zeus' ire.
I thought they'd appreciate this information
But Zeus took it as an abomination.
He chained me up, he thought forever
And commanded an eagle to peck out my liver.

Are they making the most of the gift I gave them?
I stole the gods' fire because I thought it would save them.
I still believe that my actions were right
But I find myself now on a mountain, bound tight.
I hope that the humans will use fire well
And that Zeus will release me - but you never can tell!
I now see the eagle flying towards me.
Is this the way that the gods must reward me?

But wait! Who is that in the near distance?
Could it be Hercules for instance?
He's grappling now with the huge flying beast
This is a hero, he deserves a great feast.
He carries me with all the strength of an ox
So why do I sense evil, trapped in a box?

Gabriel Nicklin (11)
Wallington County Grammar School

Hamster

Finger biter,
Food eater,
Human lover,
Cage hater.

Water drinker
Paper shredder,
Ground digger,
Ball roller.

Gap squeezer,
Fast runner,
Race winner,
Music listener,

Wall climber,
Bar swinger,
Early waker,
Night sleeper.

Sam Christy (11)
Wallington County Grammar School

Friendships

You make friends as well as lose them
I made eight and lost one
True friends are hard to find
But they last a long time
True friends are a pleasure
They are life-long treasures.

Jaabir Bhogadia (11)
Wallington County Grammar School

War

Soldiers are marching in a line
Some for revenge
Some for no reason
Some are forced
Everyone is scared and trembling in their shoes
They do not know what perilous tasks they face
They will not be able to question why
They will follow orders
And will cross many borders
Many towns and cities will perish
Many loved ones will be brutally bruised
Many loved ones will be lost
Many lives will be changed forever
For some there will be no future
For some their minds will not be complete
Civilians and soldiers alike
Does this all make it right?
Lots of noises, *bang, bang, bang! Boom, boom, boom!*
Tahir Shivji (11)
Wallington County Grammar School

My School

At last it's all over, I can't explain my relief.
The hardest thing I've ever had to go through
But finally the struggle is over.
I am victorious, I am successful.
The worst thing is I know I'll have to do it all over again
I'll have to go through all that pain again
I'll have to endure all that suffering all over again.
The tears began to stream down my face,
God, I hate leaving school . . .
Anthony Daniel (11)
Wallington County Grammar School

Food, Food, Glorious Food

Food, food, glorious food
We eat every day
We're not like other animals
We eat more types of food than they

We eat to live
If we don't we'll die
We get vitamins and minerals from food
An example is a pie

Foods can be cold
Foods can be hot
Foods can be nice
Otherwise they're not

Water has no taste
But it covers most of the planet
We all need water
Without it we would doubt it

There are many types of food that I know of
Too many to say
Some nice, some not
Would you ever not have food for one whole day?

Ahmed Suleman (11)
Wallington County Grammar School

Prometheus's Punishment

I lie here chained on the mountain top
By Zeus, my evil brother.
My mind is everywhere,
This punishment isn't fair!

The eagle's horrid pecking
Haunts me every day.
If only I could die
Like those poor, pathetic mortals.
Oh how I wish I was a mortal!

I watch the eagle seek me out,
Ready to peck my liver out.
Every day it comes for more,
While he, Zeus, watches in pleasure.

I wonder and regret why on Earth,
I gave those helpless humans fire.
I wonder what he has in store for them,
I wonder what more he has for me.

Oh no, not the wretched eagle . . .

Nandu Sanilkumar (11)
Wallington County Grammar School

The Session

Down Rose Walk I slowly thud
To start Wallington's Rugby Club.

Through the barrier of deodorant and sweat
And into the changing room I step.

Bodies fill the small, dark room
And then I see my mates in the gloom.

Then out to the pitch we jog
Escaping from the steamy fog.

Rugby balls and tackle pads
And crashing in go all the lads.

Pass! Pass! Pass it here
'I mustn't drop it,' I breathe in fear.

Now it's time for tackling
We stand in line, nervous cackling.

After much mayhem, hard work and pain
We race back to school to escape the rain.

What a rugby training session
I can't wait till the next lesson.

I wave goodbye to all my mates
And walk out through the school gates.

Harry Wrightson (12)
Wallington County Grammar School

Tornado

Tornado is a spinning inferno,
It comes with lightning and thunder.
We can just pray for it to stop,
It is in Mother Nature's control.

It is a killer,
And it is uncontrollable.
A monster of its own calibre,
Just like a murderer.

But it is also an amazing thing,
It's cold and hot air mixed together.
Blowing everything in its way,
Just like a twister who is its sister.

You're so mesmerised by it,
That you get caught up in its web.
It sucks you up like a vacuum,
Then spits you out like a camel.

Before it comes,
There is an eerie silence.
When it's gone
There's a deadly silence.

Ghalib Zaidi (12)
Wallington County Grammar School

The Tyrannosaurus Rex!

'Roar,' cries the massive beast
As it thunders through the trees,
Crushing plants under its feet
And scattering all the leaves.

It lumbers on through the wood,
Sniffing in the air;
Its eyes searching for something, but
Going close, no one will dare.

Slowly, it continues its rampage,
Through enormous jungles.
It sends a tree crashing down;
At its strength, everyone marvels.
Suddenly, it begins to run;
The smell is growing near.
It looks anxious, it looks hungry,
Everyone hides out of fear.

Its teeth gnash, its eyes narrow -
It makes your heart sink to your toes.
Its claws grasp the blazing ground,
Smoke curls up your nose.

Its skin alight with blazing flames,
They flicker, they flutter, they churn;
But as it nears you, you're filled with fright;
It's you that fire will burn!

Do you stand and fight this beast,
In all his massive terror?
Or will you leave it all alone,
To bask in its fiery lair?
Who is this you might ask?
Why of course, it is the Tyrannosaurus rex!

John Sing-Key (12)
Wallington County Grammar School

Scramble On The 463

A glint of red comes into sight
And edges slowly forwards.
It lumbers onward; no one moves.
Advances steadily; no one moves,
Heads turn to check the number.
The indicator's flashing; still no one moves,
Tickets rustle, money jingles.
It lurches to a stop: *Charge!*

And suddenly, shoving, jostling giants
Thrusting money, flashing tickets,
Elbowing, diving, pitching forwards,
Rushing for the last empty seat.
Screaming, shouting, loud disputes,
Bags flying, contents scattered.

A sudden jolt, the wheels start turning
Sliding, tumbling, toppling boys
'Hurry up! Sit down! Be quiet!'
Jokes are heard within,
Paper missiles, flying sweets,
Glances down at watches.

The time flies by, people start to leave
Pressing the bell, picking up bags
Waving and calling to friends.
It screeches to a halt, the doors creak open
I file my way out slowly,
Walk off, shouting, 'Thank you.'
And knowing that tomorrow,
I'll do it all once more!

Jonathan Mayo (11)
Wallington County Grammar School

The Conscious Prince

World;
Why are you so big?
To you
I'm just like a meaningless twig.

Sea;
That which is endless blue,
Waltzing in the wind,
Looking forever fresh and new.

Forest;
Why are your trees so wise?
With a river of flowing wisdom,
Like a heaven in disguise . . .

City;
You scavenge to quench your greed
Why not search for wisdom
Just like the trees.

Man;
Destroyer of all things beautiful and bright,
Clear your melancholy minds of darkness
To release the light.

Flower;
So beautiful and rich,
But yet you wither,
To the winter's cold witch.

Grain of sand;
Your worthlessness makes me wince,
Become a great, shining beach
And so commands your prince.

Akil Scafe-Smith (11)
Wallington County Grammar School

The Seven Stages Of Man

Life is like a poem forever casting beautifully,
There are also the seven stages of man to life,
We all are born and we all die.

First we are born and we puke a lot of times,
For hours and hours we sleep.

Next in line we become a whining schoolboy,
Who doesn't like to get away?
For him the night is the best time,
Like a cat moving stealthily along.

Next in life is the young teenager,
He falls in love for the first time
Never to forget it.

He is now a young man,
Arguing to his general in battle,
He has grown a beard and is ready for battle.

He has gone out of that stage and is now a judge,
The fair, round belly of justice is now taking a trial.

He is now an old man,
Wearing spectacles and a hearing aid.
He has also shrunk and his manly voice
has changed into a childish voice.

The next thing he sees is a brownish soil,
A worm comes and crawls into his eye!

Vishnu Jayarajan (11)
Wallington County Grammar School

Hurricane Charley

The anxiety and nerves, the fear
On the day of Hurricane Charley
Out to stock up on water and food
Fearing the worst.

First hit by Charley, Port Charlotte
To the west.
Though everyone evacuated
The thrill of the roller coaster replaced.

Moving rapidly inland she grew stronger.
Never had one moved so far.
Worse, nothing could survive the sheer power
Of Hurricane Charley.

Sitting anxiously watching the weather news.
The swishing and swirling
She let us know she was here.

Trees being battered, taken out of their roots.
Falling through villas and houses,
Tipping aeroplanes,
destroying everything in her path.

There I sat in my villa in Orlando
Hugging a pillow
Never had I been so terrified.

Time moving slowly by, we were fine
An experience and a terror
To be passed down the years
To the grandchildren.

As Charley moved on to destroy other places
Our terror was over
I was fortunate, some weren't.
Natural disaster in the state of Florida.

Matthew Scola (12)
Wallington County Grammar School

School

You go to school almost every day
And some tough work may bring dismay,
But as long as you try your best,
School will bring no test.

Learn, learn and learn some more,
Don't just sit staring at the door,
Don't drop below par,
And you'll always get an A star.

For that is what you want from school,
To be the best, not the fool
And soon you'll be revising, sat down
With nothing but a big frown.

So start studying now and you will see,
GCSE results will bring lots of glee,
So listen to me now,
So you won't get in a row
With your parents,
When you get bad marks in a test.

When you join secondary school,
Don't be a fool,
Hit the ground running
And you'll have a great time.

So take my advice
And study hard now,
Then you'll stay at the top of the class
And you'll not be the fool.

Gogulan Karunanithy (12)
Wallington County Grammar School

Life

All of life is a rugby match,
Full of struggles, miseries and joyful times,
Everyone is a player in their own game
Life is divided into eight stages.

First, birth of a new player making his debut,
Screaming and vomiting as well,
Smiling at what pleases him,
Making an impression unintentionally.

Then the walking, talking toddler,
Adventurous by nature,
With the stair-gate as their latest challenge.

The third stage, the lazy fullback, the schoolboy,
Always there to save the day,
Loitering on his own, 22,
Waiting for the ball to come to him.

Half-time, rugby number two priority,
First, well you can guess, first time love.

Then the captaincy, no time for family,
Schedule reads: interview, match interview, training,
To him he is superior to everyone.

Now the heavy prop,
Yet wise and cautious in tackles, kicks and moves,
Now his experience tells all.

His eyesight now deteriorating,
He has shrunk, now his old kit is too baggy,
As the match comes to its final stage,
His legs can't take it anymore, neither can his body,
Every second is more precious than a pot of gold.

The whistle is blown for the last time,
Dead. If you have won, that is for you to decide.

Muhammad Jaffer (11)
Wallington County Grammar School

Water And Fire!

First comes the tidal wave,
Standing high and wide,
Feared throughout the city,
But not scared by anything, anywhere,
It grows steadily preparing to attack
And when ready begins to rapidly fall,
After unleashing its ferocious power,
In the city there is nothing . . .

Then comes the volcano,
Hiding quietly and sneakily,
The city wonders what will happen,
When will it strike, when will it kill?
As the volcano begins to crumble,
The city runs in anxiety,
After exterminating the peace,
In the city there is nothing, there is no one.

Jonathan Evans (11)
Wallington County Grammar School

Wallington County Grammar School

When I first came to Wallington I had much hope,
But within a week my eyes were dropping,
I was struggling to cope.
The late nights and early mornings,
I tried hard to keep myself from yawning.
I kept up with homework, but only just about
Lessons were demanding, I was always in doubt.
Fortunately I got into the swing of how things were done,
That I got to do my best, no matter how long the run.
Now I have some spare time and I am progressing,
I got my first 'A', 3 merits and I'm not stressing.
I also have made some friends
I just hope my luck will be enough to see me to the end.

Laurence Kelly (11)
Wallington County Grammar School

Take-Off To War

The deafening plane hurtled down the runway
As if in panic, under pursuit.
Fumes, smoke and flames coming from its rear,
Roaring like a lion, making it impossible to hear.
Screeching and wailing, it lifted off the ground.

Fast as a thunderbolt, soaring like an eagle,
Like a silver bird, up towards the clouds.
Further away it glided, with its deadly load,
Safely concealed beneath the metal hood.

Smaller and smaller it became,
Leaving a trail of breath written across the sky.
It flew into a cloud, enveloped in a blanket
And disappeared, this beast of war,
The mission had begun.

Matthew Bieda (11)
Wallington County Grammar School

Wallington County Grammar School

When I first arrived at Wallington, I had butterflies inside
The boys were gigantic, the school like a maze
Blowing things up in chemistry,
Writing in English,
Problems in maths,
All of these I was looking forward to doing.

My favourite part of the day would have to be lunch,
For the pizza, chips and burgers, I could eat in a crunch.
Break time was good, footballs flying everywhere
And so were conversations I had with my friends.

The day was through, after all of my work was done,
Out of the school gates I came, I broke into a run;
'Oh no, I've missed it.' The bus had gone
'I'll have to wait for another one.'

Josh Adams (11)
Wallington County Grammar School

What If? And Have You?

What if the world was flat,
What if we all lived in a hat,
What if Johnny Wilkinson was a cat?

Have you ever seen a dog which was orange?
Have you ever seen a green orange?
Have you ever seen a child that doesn't whinge?

What if pigs could fly,
What if I was a fly,
What if Chewits made you high?

Have you never been ill?
Have you ever been called Will?
Have you ever seen a giant's hill?

What if men gave birth to babies,
What if you and me had rabies,
What if we were cabbies?

Have you ever been really dumb?
Have you ever punched your mum?
Have you ever drunk some rum?

Haaris Lone (12)
Wallington County Grammar School

The Roller Coaster

R iding through a tunnel
O verlooking the land
L ittle dots of people
L ooking round
E ven getting higher
R eady for the plunge

C hildren shaking anxiously,
O thers looking at the ground,
A s all the screams begin
S inking feeling as we drop
T hen we plunge into darkness
E veryone in shock
R appearing we gasp for air

T hen without warning, we stop
E ven then in shock we fall
R iding down vertically
R ight then we stop
O thers gaze into nothing
R eappearing we stop in one piece.

Thomas Tawse (11)
Wallington County Grammar School

Skellig

I walked into the garage and saw him there,
Like he was lifeless,
He always stared,
He said he wanted 27 and 53,
Every time he would ask me,
He didn't move, not even an inch,
Every time I saw him,
He did not flinch,
I wanted him to leave,
To fly away,
I never thought he would one day,
In the danger house he took me high,
Then he took me into the sky,
Spinning around, growing wings,
I don't know how I get into these things,
Does he have any feelings?
What is he? Where did he come from?
How old is he? What did he do to me?
Him, being known as Skellig?

Samuel Lewis (11)
Wallington County Grammar School

The Shadow

Lurking in the darkness,
Of an alley or empty street
There lies a growing evil,
You'll never want to meet.
It waits there in the mist
And as the victim draws near,
The creature's motive becomes quite clear.
Now it stalks its victim,
As close as it can get,
Making sure its victim is breaking quite a sweat.
Now the pace has quickened,
But the creature still keeps up.
Yet the man just keeps on running,
So the creature does it too.
The man is annoyed now,
He whirls round to find it's only his
Shadow!

Joshua Heath (11)
Wallington County Grammar School

Poem Of Friendship

We win some, we lose some,
I won eight and I lost one,
I was at the first day,
When we were out to play,
He began to say,
'Let's go to the library,'
And I said, 'Nay, I want to play.'
Thus I could see,
That he was angry with me,
So he walked away.

He could see,
That he lost me badly,
So fortunately,
Again he made friends with me,
By saying he was sorry,
Oh how the sky is blue,
This story is true,
Alas, he meant it never,
We will remain best friends forever.

Mohammed Kaba (11)
Wallington County Grammar School

Skellig

As I entered the garage,
I saw him there.
He glanced at me,
He truly didn't care.

I brought him food,
27 and 53.
He sat there dying,
Never once looked at me.

Was he made from
My imagination
Or was he just
A peculiar hallucination?

He alleviated joy,
Returned the one I love.
He soared away,
As elegantly as a dove.

The owls provided him strength,
I don't know how.
But he's vanished now.

Devis Kawuki (11)
Wallington County Grammar School

Michael's Story

At home I've discovered this man in our garage,
I want him kept secret, but I don't think I'll manage.
I'm sure he has wings where his shoulders should be,
But I don't want to ask him, I'll just try and see.

My little sister, her little heart,
Why does it always stop and start?
My poor mum has been so sad,
I wish I could help her, it makes me feel bad.

Dad is the same, I hate seeing him cry,
But he's so upset, he keeps shouting, 'Why?'
I'm sure the man can help us, but I don't know how,
I'll just have to try and keep patient now.

I think I'll tell Mina, the girl down the street,
As she's good with birds, I'll get them to meet.
Now Mina has met him and found Skellig's his name,
We've helped him get stronger and the baby the same.

She's no longer ill, but at home with us here,
I'm sure Skellig helped her, but it's not at all clear.
Skellig's got to leave now, I wish it wasn't so,
But he's made his decision, it's time for him to go.

Andrew James (11)
Wallington County Grammar School

The Stages Of Man

The entire world's a book,
With chapters to it,
All the men and women just characters,
They are introduced and taken away,
There are 8 stages of life.
First the baby sobbing in his mother's arms.
Then the schoolboy hating his mornings,
With his shiny face walking to school.
Then the love maker taming the girls,
Attracting them towards him.
Then the *independent* man,
Looking after himself, thinking ahead.
The Dad playing with his juniors,
Teaching them things of wisdom.
Then the man with the walking stick,
With his wrinkly face telling stories of his youth.
Secondly, the man whose energy is low,
Feeble and childlike having other people looking after him.
Finally *death* the last and crucial stage of life,
Nothing is heard.

Umar Ghulab
Wallington County Grammar School

The School

The school playground, the school playground
What a confusing place to be.

All these different playgrounds and I'm trying
To discover which one's for me.

The school canteen, the school canteen,
Oh what a wonderful smell.

They sell chips, pizza and even sausage rolls
People push in front like they're urging you to tell.

The school halls, the school halls
Like an alleyway of doors.

All the same colour, you wonder which one's yours.
Everyone trying to get to their class, barging you back and forth.

But later on you get used to that, it happens regularly . . .
Wallington school, Wallington school
You might be sad because you're leaving your friends,
But trust me it's worth it.

Terory Larebo (11)
Wallington County Grammar School

My Days At Wallington

When I arrived at Wallington
I was already tired!
Although I hadn't done any lessons yet,
My eyes were weighed down with tons of new images.

In the Induction days
I got a chance to make some friends
Which made it easier in September.
My head ached from trying to remember all their names!

We had PE, then lunch.
Starving, we waited patiently in the snaking queue.
After, we went to the playground
With full stomachs we were ready for the afternoon timetable.

So here I am, I've survived a month
My eyes are used to new places,
My head puts names to faces
But my stomach still rumbles in that snaking queue!

Michael Eglon (12)
Wallington County Grammar School